PRAISE FOR LORILYN ROBERTS

"I resonated deeply with many of these stories—tears flowing freely. There's nothing like the comfort of a warm fuzzy kitten or a loyal, loving dog when you are feeling down, alone, or devastated."
~Carol A. Brown, *author of Christian adult nonfiction and children's animal stories*

"**Sure to be a hit with the 'I love animals' crowd.**"
~*Michael J. Webb, author of cutting-edge Christian fiction and inspiring nonfiction*

"**I wholeheartedly loved the book.**"
~*Darla Abney-Cox, Amazon Reader*

TAILS AND PURRS FOR THE HEART AND SOUL

LORILYN ROBERTS

Rear Guard Publishing, Inc.

Copyright © 2020 Lorilyn Roberts

Rear Guard Publishing, Inc.

Gainesville, FL 32606

Ver 1.0

Cover photograph – standard licensing agreement

Cover design by Lisa Vento

Edited by Lisa Lickel

All rights reserved. No part of this book may be reproduced or utilized in any form or by any means, electronic or mechanical, or by any information storage retrieval system except for brief quotations for the purpose of review without written permission from the publisher.

Unless otherwise noted, all Scripture is taken from the King James Version, public domain.

Scripture quotations marked (NLT) are taken from the Holy Bible, New Living Translation, copyright © 1996, 2004, 2007, 2013, 2015 by Tyndale House Foundation. Used by permission of Tyndale House Publishers, Inc., Carol Stream, Illinois 60188. All rights reserved.

Scripture quotations taken from The Holy Bible, New International Version NIV Copyright © 1973, 1978, 1984, 2011 Biblica, Inc., Used by permission.

Scripture quotations are from The ESV® Bible (The Holy Bible, English Standard Version®), copyright © 2001 by Crossway, a publishing ministry of Good News Publishers. Used by permission. All rights reserved.

Scriptures marked TLB are taken from THE LIVING BIBLE (TLB): Scripture taken from THE LIVING BIBLE copyright© 1971. Used by permission of Tyndale House Publishers, Inc., Carol Stream, Illinois 60188. All rights reserved.

Library of Congress Control Number: 2020918880

ISBN: 978-1-7339989-1-8 (e-book)

ISBN: 978-1-7339989-2-5 (print, Am)

ISBN: 978-1-7339989-3-2 (print, LS)

Printed and bound in the United States of America

DEDICATION

All the dogs and cats

*that have left their mark on my family's heart
and soul*

Gypsy
Gretchen
Tasha
Noah
Shelley
Fifi
Rex
Abbey
Thomasina
Boots (on the back cover)
Tinkerbell
James
Lewis
Lily
Molly
Sirius
Twila
Anakin
Kenobi
Faye
Gracie
Kitty
Sweet Pea
Peppi
Much Afraid (Israel)

CONTENTS

Prologue	1
1. Grief That Has No Name	5
2. Six Years Old	9
3. Eight Years Old	11
4. My Best Friend, Gypsy	14
5. The Slipper	20
6. Gretchen	23
7. My Promise	28
8. Tasha	31
9. Shelley	43
10. Fifi	48
11. Bugs and Furry Felines	56
12. Beach Trip with Shelley	59
13. The Vision	64
14. I Want to Sing	67
15. Rex	70
16. No Record	76
17. Gypsy - Never Give Up	78
18. "Much Afraid"	81
19. Baruch	86
20. Mother's Day, May 8 1994	91
21. More Stories About Rex	95
22. Abbey	99
23. Thomasina	105
24. Molly Part 1	110
25. Molly Part 2	115
26. Boots and Tinkerbell	120
27. Lily and Sirius	126
28. Sirius' Shenanigans	133
29. Sirius' Escapades	140
30. The Great Adventure	145
31. Sirius' Guardian Angel	149

32. Possums and More	154
33. Twila	163
34. Lewis and James	168
35. Anakin	174
36. Kenobi	179
37. Faye	185
38. One Happy Family	190
39. Kenobi's Accident	194
40. Breast Cancer	199
41. The Flying Cat	202
42. Anakin's Emergency	205
43. Proton Therapy	210
44. Life After Cancer	215
45. Alaska	219
46. Sirius	224
47. Hard Times	228
48. Providence	232
49. Kenobi	236
50. A Broken Heart	239
51. Healing in the Garden	244
52. James Part 2	249
53. Healing of the Heart	255
54. Adoption	259
55. Gracie	262
56. All in the Family	269
57. Sweet Pea	276
Epilogue	284
Notes	287
Also by Lorilyn Roberts	288
About the Author	291

PROLOGUE

Years ago, while driving home from Flagler Beach, I got stuck at the only traffic light in the small Florida town of Bunnell. The rural area in Northeast Florida probably has more deer than people.

No one was on the road, and as I waited impatiently for the light to turn green, a familiar feeling came over me. I had experienced it several times over the past year, but I couldn't identify it.

I wasn't going through a crisis. No heavy burdens bore down on my shoulders. Since I wasn't working overtime, I'd had enough spare time to spend a Saturday afternoon jumping waves at the beach.

I thought about my recently finalized divorce. Was I still grieving? Why would I want to remarry the cheater who left me?

Was it because I wanted to be closer to my family? I loved my family, but I didn't want to move back to Atlanta.

Was it because I wanted to return to The University of Florida and finish my bachelor's? That made the most sense because I disliked my career as a court reporter.

Or could it be all those things?

I pleaded with God, "Help me to figure this out."

A short time later, I discovered the great Christian author C. S. Lewis. In a documentary, he talked about longing. I wanted to jump out of my chair when I heard the following quote: "If I find in myself desires which nothing in this world can satisfy, the only logical explanation is that I was made for another world."

That was it. I was longing for heaven. Why did I not experience this desire before my divorce? As I thought about it, I knew. In my youthful foolishness, I had sought worldly things. I put my ex-husband through medical school and looked forward to the day I'd have a house with a pool and a brand-new car.

God knew better than to give me those worldly idols. After being humbled, the Holy Spirit took away my love for this world and replaced it with a longing for the next. As I reflected, contentment swallowed up my anxious spirit. I'd never heard anybody describe this longing for heaven. However, if C. S. Lewis had it, then I must not be weird.

I began to read books by this unique theologian. I'd wanted to be an author in my younger years. Maybe someday I could inspire others in the same way Lewis had inspired me.

C. S. Lewis died on November 22, 1963, the same day President John F. Kennedy was assassinated. I was only eight years old, and it would be decades after C. S. Lewis' death that I would even know who he was.

C. S. Lewis was a deep thinker, and few people like him are willing to ask profound or even troubling questions. I seem to have a habit of coming up with my own.

For example, does God mean for us to be unfulfilled here until we enter the celestial city? It seems ungodlike to bestow longings on people if their only fulfillment is in a distant world. Perhaps the complete realization is later, but what about now?

Since that longing is an eternal desire, perhaps God wants to whet our appetite here. Could that mean God has put something inside each of us to point us to heaven? In the meantime, while we "occupy," could our joy in Him compel us to live better than we would if we only lived for ourselves?

In the beginning, the very beginning, God gave Adam a perfect helpmate—Eve. God made Eve before there was any sin in the garden.

When Eve ate the fruit that God told Adam and Eve not to eat, sin entered the world. To this day, Satan desires to thwart the perfect plan of the Creator. But God isn't limited. If plan A doesn't work out, God has a plan B or a backup plan.

In some cases, plan B might even be better. No matter how sanctified we are, we can't escape the grim reality of the lost Garden of Eden, but God always has a plan. He never abandons us.

Something else in the Genesis account often gets overlooked. Before God created woman, He brought all the birds, animals, and beasts to Adam. He named the creatures God brought to him. God hoped that one of them would be "fit" to be Adam's helpmate. When the perfect helpmate wasn't found, God created Eve.

Plan A, in my case, was a disaster. So God went with plan B and blessed me with many furry friends. They have been my helpmates in times of joy, grief, and uncertainty. While a few sections of *Tails and Purrs for the Heart and Soul* might more accurately be described as memoir, my reason for including them is to give context to the fullness of joy and how my animal friends have blessed me.

Indeed, God has given me many "helpers," and if I don't share these stories, I'll always wish I did. God has assured me I'll see my furry friends again. God is good even when we doubt, and that eternal longing for heaven can be sweet to the heart and soul even while we wait for our future home.

So get ready to read about the face mask thief, turtle rattlers, heroic acts of devotion, and God's providence when my soul cried and my heart ached—you won't be disappointed.

I

GRIEF THAT HAS NO NAME

"I want it all, and I want it now," the television ad blared. I didn't have to caption commercials, so I released my fingers from the stenograph keyboard, sat back, and gazed at the T.V. screen. I'd been a broadcast captioner for twenty years. I'd seen thousands of commercials, but the bonehead message of this one grated on my heart even more. I only wanted one thing.

I bowed my head as tears rolled down my cheeks. It wasn't the commercial that ate at my soul. I turned my eyes to the dresser on the wall adjacent to my desk. A newly-placed, engraved wooden container holding my beloved cat's ashes sat prominently in view. I'd just brought Kenobi home in the box, the cremated remains of my five-year-old black and white feline.

I'd lost animals before—when most of them lived to a ripe, old age, and nature took its predictable course. But never one this young who deserved so much more, never one who was as sweet and loving as he.

"Why, God?" But God didn't answer.

"Kenobi," I whispered through my tears, "I miss you so much. I would've done anything I could to save you; if only I could have."

My show returned, and I thumped my fingers on the keyboard. Thanks to broadcast captioning, the deaf would "hear." But my mind was on my broken heart.

I remembered Ecclesiastes 1:14: "I have seen all the things that are done under the sun, all of them are meaningless, a chasing after the wind" (NLT).

Is this all there is to life, a chasing after the wind? I couldn't think about anything but my cat. The throbbing pain was so raw, so biting—we'd lost three pets in the last year—and my grief bore into my heart like cancer.

As we lost each one, I'd thank God, even in my pain, "At least Kenobi is still with us." We didn't expect him to live much longer.

I'd have to learn how to live again—like after breast cancer three years earlier. I was tired of learning how to live again. Was life even worth living? I clenched my eyes to focus on my captions.

I could write just about anything flawlessly, but tonight was a struggle. I wept as flashes of Kenobi flooded my mind. I replayed his sudden appearance from the bedroom, pulling his paralyzed legs behind him, his heart-throbbing cry for help, and my panic attack that followed.

"Oh, Lord, why did you have to take him? Why, God?"

I tried to minimize my grief. Others had suffered far more than me—a lot more. But I didn't care about anyone else's pain. I only cared about mine.

Right then, I made up my mind. I would never take in another homeless animal. I'd never love another dog, cat, bird—nothing. I'd never risk being hurt again. My heart was too broken to adopt any more animals, or rescue any more needy pets, or pour my heart into a hurting four-legged creature that might not live but a short time.

I'd love the animals I already had, and once the last of them went to their final resting place, I'd throw away the key to my heart so nothing could ever break it again. I couldn't take the pain. I couldn't look into the eyes of another beloved pet and tell him I couldn't help him.

2

SIX YEARS OLD

I remember the first time a cat made its dramatic entrance into my life. We had recently moved into a cheap apartment on the second floor up a steep wooden stairway. I discovered that a cat lived in the first-floor apartment beneath us. Every time we came home, I'd look at that closed door, hoping to get a sneak peek inside. Someone told me cats purred—someone older than me, and almost everybody was older than me when I was six.

One day Mother needed to run errands, so she dropped me off at the cat apartment. To be in the same house with a purring cat unlocked many possibilities. I asked the young boy who lived there if I could see the cat. He went on an all-out search to find the four-legged furry feline.

Did the cat believe I might cat snatch him? Is that why the critter disappeared? After a few minutes of detective work, the boy, who was about my age, reappeared holding the annoyed critter. I perked up my ears to hear the expected "meow."

Suddenly the upset creature hissed.

"Ooh!" I didn't expect that.

The boy warned, "Don't get too close, or he'll scratch you."

Ignoring his warnings, I stuck my ear right up to the feline as close as I dared, but all I heard was another loud hiss. The terrified animal jumped out of the boy's arms and scrambled up the stairs.

"What are you doing to that poor cat?" the boy's mother scolded as she entered the living room.

"We wanted to hear him purr," he said.

"Leave the cat alone." The upset mother glanced at me. "He doesn't like strangers."

I was so disappointed.

3
EIGHT YEARS OLD

One morning I awoke from a fantasy world more thrilling than Disney could ever create. I felt a wet, warm kiss on my cheek. When I opened my eyes and saw a dog, I wrapped my arms around her.

"Who are you?" I asked. As my dreamy eyes focused, I saw she was white, and somehow, she had walked into the house, run up the stairs, and found me in bed.

My mother stood across from me with a smile etched across her face.

I patted the dog's head. "Where did she come from?"

"This is Gypsy. We're going to keep her," she said.

I blinked to make sure I hadn't died and gone to heaven. Not that I even knew where that was, but I wanted to make sure I wasn't starring in a Hollywood movie. Surely this was just make-believe.

A prominent movie director in New York once tried to convince my mother to let him take me to Hollywood. My mother said no, and I lost my only bid for Hollywood stardom. Instead, Hollywood discovered Hayley Mills. Everybody, when I was young, compared me to her. I've heard it said everybody has a twin. Hayley Mills was mine.

Everything faded into the bedroom walls as I focused on the bouncy white, playful pearl. While some might argue we saved her from a wretched life on the streets, I'd say she saved me from a very challenging, lonely childhood. Is dog not God spelled backward? Mother told me how the night before, Gypsy snuck into the apartment through the door with my stepfather—who I call Dad for the remainder of the book—when he returned from the store to buy milk.

Soon Gypsy became my faithful companion and playmate. When I came home from school, she would be waiting for me at the door. I invented games to play with her. I would place my hand underneath the blanket and move it around, and Gypsy would "fetch" it with her mouth. I soon learned how much dogs love to chew on shoes, slippers, and record covers.

When I came home from school, I could hardly wait to walk her. When we returned after each walk, I would announce how many times Gypsy had used the bathroom, both number one and number two, to validate I was the best dog walker in the world. I cleaned up after her when she made a mess so nobody would know. I always had a deep-seated fear I might lose her.

One afternoon I arrived home from school, and I knew something was wrong. Gypsy didn't greet me at the door, and I ran through the house looking for her.

"She's gone," my mother told me. "The apartment manager said we couldn't keep her, and your father took her to a protected area. Don't worry. She'll be fine."

"Where did he take her?"

My mother paused before continuing. "You know the apartment complex doesn't allow dogs. We had no choice."

My heart broke. I knew it might come to this. I'd overheard the whispers. I ran out of the room and up the stairs to my bedroom. Burying my face in the pillow, I cried. Gypsy was gone. I didn't want to believe I would never see her again. Even at eight, I believed in miracles.

That night thunderbolts crashed outside my bedroom, and lightning pierced through the window shades. I imagined Gypsy in the darkness. I could feel her fur against my skin and see her dark, brown eyes pleading for me. I twisted and turned in bed as peals of thunder bounced off the walls. If Gypsy ever found her way back, I vowed to run away with her. I would never let anybody take her from me again.

The next day came and went. She didn't return. I went to school, hoping she would find her way back.

After another stormy night, Wednesday arrived, the day before Thanksgiving. We were packing things to visit my new father's family in North Carolina. My mother had recently remarried. We had yet to meet the extended family of her new husband—a brother and three sisters.

I kept looking up the hill in front of the apartment, imagining that I would see my dog come flying over the rise in the road. I knew it was almost impossible, but I hoped. I made one last trip to my bedroom. The car was loaded, and we were ready to leave. I picked up my pillow and remembered the first morning Gypsy awoke me and licked me on the face.

"God, please help Gypsy to find her way back."

I walked out the door to get into the car. Glancing one last time up the hill, I saw something white. Was it, could it be—I dropped my pillow and started to run. My mind raced, and I ran as fast as my legs would move. It couldn't be—but it was.

Tattered and dirty and barking excitedly, Gypsy ran toward me, flashing her tail in the wind. She had survived two nights of bad weather and found her way home through a raging storm. If she had arrived two minutes later, we would have been on the road.

I crouched down and held her as she whimpered and licked my face. I didn't know I could laugh and cry at the same time, but one thing I did know—God brought Gypsy back to me.

"I will never let go of you," I promised.

Gypsy squealed.

For the first time, I believed in God.

4

MY BEST FRIEND, GYPSY

G ypsy was a medium-sized, white dog with brown spots on her back. When I peered into her brown eyes, I saw unconditional love. God blessed her with soft fur that never quit shedding. Her ears flipped forward naturally, and her body was feminine and delicate. Her foot-long fluffy tail would flash like a swishy broom when she wagged it. Her gentle face looked similar to a Samoyed, but she did not have the build of an Eskimo dog that could pull a sled. She was only half the size of a full-grown Samoyed if even that.

I've often wondered what she was a mixture of because she didn't look like any breed. When I traveled internationally, like Nepal, Vietnam, Italy, and Israel, I'd see dogs that reminded me of her.

Gypsy was a happy dog. She was also sweet, affectionate, and smart—I mean, brilliant, with a keen sense of smell that led to some magical feats of heroism.

After Mom and Dad decided to keep her, despite the threat of eviction, we needed to take her to the vet to get checked out, but she was too afraid to get into the car. We had to coax her. Gypsy needed medication for her mangy skin, and, of course, the required rabies and distemper shots.

Mom faithfully applied the ointment to her skin. After a few months, the mange went away, transforming her into a beautiful dog. After a couple of trips to the vet, Gypsy got used to Dad's old white 1962 Chevy, and then she couldn't get enough of the car. She was ready for a trip anytime we would take her.

Back in those days, gas was cheap, and since our family didn't have any money, we would go on drives into the country for fun. I remember a couple of times getting stuck in the boonies. I learned how to get a stuck car unstuck long before I learned how to drive.

Frequently, we would take Gypsy with us. She loved to plant her paws on the windowsill, stick her head out the window as the wind buffeted her head, and watch the world pass by. Her nose would be going faster than the car—and sheer joy enveloped her enraptured soul.

My main chore was to walk her. That was probably the only chore I ever enjoyed. It sure beat putting out the glass milk bottles to be picked up by the milkman twice a week. That's how people got their milk back in those days.

I'd walk Gypsy all over the apartment complex to show off my best friend. Much to the apartment manager's disdain, I made it a point to walk by her door as if daring her to take Gypsy away. I wouldn't let that happen.

I'm sure the grumpy ole woman wanted to evict us, but we would be moving out soon anyway. Mom and Dad had bought some property north of Atlanta in Cobb County, and we were building a house. The only question was whether we would move out before the manager kicked us out.

We made many trips to Marietta over the next year. Because the area was so rural, we'd let Gypsy wander the countryside. In the meantime, we sat on bricks stacked up in the Georgia red clay, surrounded by building materials galore, and sipped on root beer and orange crush during the hot summer.

Slowly our future house took shape. I loved those trips away from Atlanta. I'd never lived anywhere except an apartment surrounded by concrete. Here there was nature and plenty of open land Gypsy and I could explore.

One time when we were ready to leave to go back to Atlanta, Gypsy didn't come when Dad called. My father said, "I think she'll come when she hears the car engine."

We took off down Bells Ferry Road, and I scanned the countryside looking for a white streak in the distance. "There she is," I shouted.

Gypsy was matching the speed of the car, stride for stride, running like a white wolf. Dad pulled off the road, and she jumped in. I mildly scolded her, "Why did you scare me? I was afraid I might not see you again."

When Mother gave birth to my sister, Gypsy spent a week in the living room corner sulking. She believed my sister had usurped her. I suppose when she realized the baby was here to stay, she needed to make the best of the situation.

When my sister was old enough to sit on the floor, Gypsy would lie beside her on the blanket. My sister would play with Gypsy's bushy tail and offer to share her pacifier. Gypsy had no qualms about taking it. She'd chew on any baby toys or pacifiers dropped on the floor. My sister didn't mind. She'd just laugh at the big white dog that entertained her, and they would both "suck" on the pacifier.

Gypsy loved to chew on lots of other things, but especially Dad's music albums. This was back when people had record players, and Dad's records were on a record stand at just the right height for Gypsy to nibble on. I still have one of those album covers. I should probably tell my daughters why it looks so ragged. They'd laugh. "Oh, Mom…" I'm too sentimental.

I learned very young that dogs are good to have around when thieves want to steal your stuff. There was a rash of stolen bikes, clothes from clotheslines, and outdoor grills from the apartment buildings surrounding us. Gypsy would bark if she heard noises outside after dark, especially in the middle of the night.

We never had anything taken from our porch, even though our neighbors did. The thief went elsewhere because of our barking dog.

I remember the day we moved into our new house. After almost a year, Gypsy was free to roam among the fields and woods around us. She was in her element, and somehow, she knew the day she would never have to go back to being chained at the apartment.

I loved Gypsy's restless spirit. I was nine when we moved, and many days Gypsy and I would go for long hikes exploring the nearby woods. She loved wandering along the leafy trails, sniffing holes, and investigating overhanging rocks to find hidden treasures.

Her wanderings drew me to God as we trekked over the rolling hills and meadows. Sometimes we'd run into sticky spider webs, but I never got used to that. At dusk, fireflies would appear, followed by pesky mosquitos. That's when we'd head home for dinner.

I don't know if I would love nature like I do today if we had not spent those memorable days together exploring the great outdoors. My family wasn't into camping or hiking or minimalism. My mother's idea of ruggedness hasn't changed in the last fifty years. She's quite content to sit on the back porch, admiring deer and turkey as she drinks coffee or hot chocolate.

I enjoy that, too, but I treasure those years when I was young hiking those uncharted lands with my faithful companion. Because Gypsy was a good guard dog, as she proved on more than one occasion, my parents never worried about me.

We shared an inseparable bond, a unique kinship. Her unconditional love inspired me, and her determination against all odds to be with me pointed to a loving, awesome Eternal Father.

As the years passed, more neighbors moved into the neighborhood, and we needed to put up a fence, especially when leash laws took effect. Gypsy hated being fenced in and would figure out how to dig out of the backyard.

Once we had a rat problem in my bedroom, or maybe it was a mouse. To me, rats and mice are all the same. We put out traps to catch the villain, but to no avail. Then one night, I was getting ready to take a shower, and the rodent ran out of the shower. I screamed in horror and ran to find Gypsy. My parents came rushing downstairs to see what was wrong.

Amid all the excitement, Gypsy ran into the bathroom, and we followed her into the tiny area. We found her standing next to the toilet, and the rat was hanging out both sides of her mouth. We clapped excitedly for her amazing feat. The scoundrel had evaded the mousetrap for months. No one knew what would happen next, whether she would play with it until she killed it or drop it on the floor. None of us expected what followed.

Gypsy juggled the critter in her mouth as it squirmed, tossed it up in the air, and in an instant, the rat slid down her throat in one long gulp. There was no blood—nothing. The last thing I saw was the flip-flopping tail hanging out of her mouth before it disappeared.

We cheered in celebration, letting her know what a wonderful deed she'd done. Our rat problem was over, and Gypsy was a hero. I did have a pang of sadness that the rodent met such an unfortunate demise. Still, I was tired of being traumatized by something that probably carried a thousand diseases.

5
THE SLIPPER

I don't think there has ever been a dog with a keener sense of smell than Gypsy. Before my mother remarried, she wanted to give her future husband a special gift as a token of her love, but everyone knew Mother had no creativity. Even a mockingbird would have had a hard time imitating her off-key singing. A poetic piece about her Prince Charming would have been a comedy at best. A delectably good steak she prepared one night had my future father reaching for the Band-Aids because it was so red.

"Let's put a Band-Aid on this cow, and we can get him on the road again," he said. Her lack of depth perception in avoiding cars in parking lots removed all doubt of being able to draw a three-dimensional romantic picture.

My mother wasn't blessed with a lot of originality, but there was one thing she could do well. She could knit. One day, Mother arrived home with her knitting needles and bundles of yarn in an assortment of colors—reds, browns, yellows and blues—and two brown soles.

"What are you going to do with that?" I asked.

"I'm going to knit a special present to give to my fiancé on our wedding day," she said.

Night after night, I watched her work tirelessly with the long blue needles moving back and forth. Slowly, a beautiful geometric shape of white and yellow diamonds emerged. Several inches of dark brown stitches tapered to the edge of the top of the slippers.

When they were almost complete, she attached the soles with strong black stitches so the slippers would never tear or come apart. After weeks of knitting, a beautiful pair of hand-made slippers emerged. Sewn with love and given to her husband on their wedding day, the slippers never lost their specialness.

One summer day after we moved into our house, we saw the neighbor's dog carrying one of the slippers into the woods. We made much effort to find the slipper the neighbor dog had stolen. A local Boy Scout troop scoured the woods. A week passed, and despite all of our best efforts, we didn't find the slipper. We kept an eye out for it the rest of the summer, but it never turned up.

The hot, humid nights of summer came and went. The autumn winds blew brightly colored orange and yellow leaves off the trees, leaving them naked and exposed. Winter rolled in, and the woods around our house were silent, gray, and cold. Snow blanketed the frozen landscape like white ivory pearls. The lost slipper was forgotten.

Spring arrived, and the harsh, gray winter receded as signs of life brought renewal. The woods around our house, adorned in the spectacular beauty of layers of white blooming dogwoods, meant hot summer days would soon follow. The whippoorwill would once again serenade us as we caught lightning bugs in peanut butter jars.

One summer evening was different from the rest. As we relaxed on the porch in the coolness of the day, we caught a glimpse of Gypsy as she ran out of the woods. At first, we didn't notice anything unusual, but as she got closer and slowed to a trot, we could see her carrying something.

The object was brown with diamond designs. Gypsy strode up with her head held high and plopped down the long, lost sandal in front of Dad, as if to say, "This belongs to you. A thief stole it, but I found it and am restoring it to you."

We stared at the slipper as it lay at Dad's feet. A year had passed since it went missing—followed by a harsh winter with snow and ice. We never knew where she found it, but that was Gypsy. She had quite a reputation for doing the impossible.

❧ 6 ❧
GRETCHEN

Gretchen

W e'd lived in our new house for a couple of years, and Gypsy spent her days when I was at school exploring the neighborhood hills. She had all the freedom for which she had longed when we lived in the apartment. She lived the life of a gypsy—until she bit the garbageman. Then we had to chain her.

Dad strung a wire across a large section of the backyard, which I promptly ran into and cut my face. I still remember that unfortunate encounter, so Dad raised the wire to save my teeth. I was wearing braces.

Gypsy didn't let the chain destroy her spirit, and she'd run across the yard as the chain slid along the wire. On more than one occasion, I asked her, "Why did you go and bite the garbageman?" If only I could have explained to her why we had to chain her. We were afraid the garbageman would call the dog catcher, and she would be hauled away. I don't know what possessed her to do that. Mother said Gypsy thought the garbageman was stealing our stuff.

As time passed, Dad took ownership of a map company and moved the business into the basement. During the day, Gypsy lounged on an old blanket underneath the large light table where Dad drew the artwork. Soon we had employees coming to work and customers coming to buy maps. It made life chaotic, plus I now had a younger brother and sister.

Even into my teenage years, Gypsy slept in my room at night, and soon she wasn't the only dog in the Roberts' household. The day came when she got a playmate. One of the employees had a litter of German Shepherd puppies, and we adopted one and named her Gretchen.

Gypsy loved being the top dog and bossed Gretchen around quite a bit—until Gretchen grew bigger than Gypsy. Somehow the two of them worked out the alpha-beta thing. I was happy when we got Gretchen because Gypsy loved having a friend.

Gretchen was almost a perfect dog. At least I thought she was until she stole the neighbor's baseball mitt. So, my parents, having a few extra dollars and wanting to be responsible neighbors, put up a fence to keep Gretchen from stealing any more baseball mitts.

Gretchen didn't dig out of the yard like Gypsy, and Gretchen was a good watchdog even if she was a thief. Despite the hundreds of people who came to the house to buy maps, we never had a single untoward incident.

One time the UPS man came to pick up some maps and forgot to ring the doorbell. It only happened once. Gretchen was Johnny-on-the-spot.

When Gretchen wasn't a guard dog, she and Gypsy would take

turns barking at squirrels, chewing on acorns, and chasing whatever animal entered our yard uninvited—except one time a dog came over and stayed a while.

Someone noticed Gretchen had put on some weight. A couple of days later, she delivered eight puppies before we even knew she was pregnant. We were never sure who the father was, but several prospects lived nearby. I guess one of them knew how to climb a fence. Of course, we've often wondered if Gypsy dug the suitor's hole and then covered up her misdeed.

A couple of years later, we bred Gretchen to our neighbor's German Shepherd—they had gotten over the baseball mitt incident—and Gretchen had thirteen puppies. By this time, the business had taken over the basement, and Dad had even enclosed the garage. Where do you put thirteen puppies and a German Shepherd? In my shower, of course. I shared a bathroom with the office staff.

Gretchen would go into the shower to do her motherly duties, and the office staff knew when Gretchen was nursing her babies. Nobody gave it any thought when a lady from Northside Realty stopped by to buy a map one day and asked to use the bathroom.

"Sure, the bathroom is over there, through the laundry room."

A minute later, the poor woman screamed and came running out of the bathroom, still trying to pull up her pants. "There is a German Shepherd in the shower," she exclaimed.

We looked at each other trying not to laugh. We'd forgotten it was nursing time.

I wanted to keep one of the puppies, but that wasn't to be. Eventually, we found homes for all of them. By that time, we'd had enough of the puppy thing. Gretchen was spayed, and that was the end of her mothering days.

With all Gypsy's escapades, I never knew how she avoided getting pregnant. We never had her fixed, but she had a favorite pillow. I guess that was her companion.

Besides being a baseball mitt thief, Gretchen had one imperfect day in her fourteen years of life. One evening we were sitting down to eat a delicious steak dinner when the doorbell rang. Someone went to the door, and the man with the brand-new electric typewriter invited us out to his car to see it.

As a young girl, I'd never seen an electric typewriter. Mother typed the business invoices on a manual Crown Royal typewriter. We all left the table and rushed outside to see the new marvel of the twenty-first century. (This was way back in the 1960s).

We stood around the old Chevy station wagon wide-eyed in awe as we inspected the state-of-the-art typewriter. After lauding the piece of modern wizardry and celebrating our forward leap into the age of technology, we returned to the table to finish our dinner.

To our shock, our well-behaved seventy-pound German Shepherd stood in the middle of the table, licking her chops. Not a scrap of food remained except steak bones.

No one said anything for a moment. We ended up eating peanut butter and jelly sandwiches. I still think about that steak dinner we never ate—probably my favorite memory of Gretchen. That was the only time she wasn't perfect. I guess she had no interest in the new electric typewriter.

Throughout all those years, Gypsy slept in my room on the floor next to my bed. She was my constant companion as I studied hard in school and later took up classical guitar. As the years passed, it never occurred to me how much she shed. I had a blue woolen coat I loved, and Gypsy's white hair stuck to it like glue. Friends would ask if we had a dog. I would proudly tell them, "Yes, I have the greatest dog in the world."

7

MY PROMISE

One day Gypsy escaped from the backyard for the first time in a while. While I worried if she was okay, I was secretly thankful she enjoyed a delightful romp as she had been fenced in for far too long. God made her a gypsy, and once again, she sniffed out the hills as she had done when we first moved to Marietta, back when we explored the nooks and crannies in the virgin woods before they were torn down and replaced with houses.

Even though we looked for her, we couldn't find her. She returned home from that adventure when she was ready. However, not long after that she began to pee in the house. My parents moved her bed from my bedroom into the utility room because of the accidents.

We made a big deal about it—that this was her new place, but I knew she wasn't happy. She reluctantly complied, and after we closed the door, I lingered, watching as she lay on her bed. I was sad that she couldn't sleep in my room anymore, but I had carpet in my bedroom, and we couldn't have her peeing on it.

If only we had known what was wrong, if only we had taken her to the vet for a urinary tract infection. She must have caught it on that final romp she took down by the retention pond, but we didn't know.

Nothing stays the same. Life changes, we change, the world

8
TASHA

Each of us grieved the loss of Gypsy in different ways. Mother began to research various breeds of dogs, and six months later, we adopted a female Samoyed named Tasha. For those unfamiliar with these magnificent animals, they're large, white, furry, working dogs with a strong herding instinct. Native to Canada, Russia, and Alaska, they have a long history dating back to the Samoyede nomads of Northwestern Siberia. Earning the trust and loyalty as a member of the tribesman's family, they used them for hunting and hauling sleds.

changes, and Gypsy changed. I sensed she was sick. I felt it in my soul. I told Dad, and he came downstairs to check on her. Gypsy pretended to be okay, perhaps not wanting to alarm Dad, but I knew she wasn't.

A couple of days later, as was my routine getting up in the morning, I went to the utility room to put her outside. When I opened the door, she was lying on the floor unresponsive. Usually, she would get up and wag her tail when she heard me approaching. I called to her, but she didn't hear me, although I could tell she was faintly breathing.

I ran upstairs to my parents' bedroom and shouted through the door that something was wrong with Gypsy. They said they would check on her in a few minutes. I had to go to school. Why couldn't they come now?

With a heavy heart, I caught the bus to school. A few hours later, I was summoned out of my government class. I packed up my books and walked into the hallway. Dad was waiting for me.

"How is Gypsy?" I asked, fearing the worst.

"She's dead," he said.

Was there nothing anyone could do for her? I cried all the way down the hallway. I wasn't sure I'd ever be happy again. Even though we still had Gretchen, no dog could replace Gypsy. She was too young to die. "Why so soon, Lord?"

Later that day, Dad dug a large hole in the backyard to bury her as I grieved alone in my bedroom. After a while—it seemed as if he had been digging for a long time—I stepped outside.

Still shaken, I saw Dad's old green bag beside the hole. He was a veteran, having served in the Air Force as an airplane mechanic during the Korean War. Then I realized, Gypsy was in the bag. In my heart, I knew how much that bag meant to Dad—a keepsake from his past before he married my mother and adopted me at ten.

It was late afternoon, perhaps closer to evening, and suddenly darkness flooded the sky. A storm blew in from nowhere. Rain began to fall, thunder clapped, and lightning shattered the sky into splinters of white daggers. Dad had the shovel in his hands and was still digging. The hole looked big enough to me. I feared lightning might strike the shovel.

The rain fell harder. Finally, Dad lifted the bag into the hole and shoveled the dirt on top.

I prayed, "Gypsy, I promise you, someday the world will know who you are and how much you mean to me. God sent you to me because He knew I needed a friend."

I looked up at the angry sky overhead as Dad finished filling in the hole.

"God brought you to me in a thunderstorm, and today He has taken you from me in a thunderstorm. I love you so much."

How would I keep my promise? I had no idea, but somehow, I would. That was back in the days when our lives only intersected with a few others—at work, school, or church. Sometimes we can say things without realizing how our words will impact others or the future. When Dad finished, we headed to the house.

Fifty years later, I still remember Gypsy with a vividness that is hard to explain. Her determination and will inspired me to never give up on my dreams. Even when we had to confine her, she found joy.

She was always seeking, always exploring, and always finding treasures, like Dad's lost slipper. I, too, cast my net wide and found two pearls of great price—beautiful souls on loan to me to raise and love. God's Word never returns void. Few know how hard I prayed to be a mother.

Sometimes I dream about Gypsy. She is all white, wagging her fluffy tail, and dancing on her tippy toes peeking around a door. She remains on the other side just beyond my reach. I imagine her exploring the spectacular vistas of heaven just as she roamed the woods near our house.

Someday I will see her loving eyes again, hold her in my arms, and hear her squeal with delight when God opens the door. Abounding in unconditional love, she taught me how to love all the other pets that someday would fill my heart.

The dogs also played an important role in helping explorers to reach the North and South Poles. In more recent years, they are famous for competing in races like the 1,100-mile Iditarod dogsled race from Anchorage to Nome, Alaska.

Mother reconnected with her past and all the fond memories she had of going to the Westminster Dog Show each year in New York. She grew up in the Brooklyn-Scarsdale area, and dog shows were in her blood. All I knew about those days was that she went with her boyfriend. I guess part of that romance was her love for dogs, too.

However, I've since learned there is more to this story. I want to share a little piece my mom wrote in 2016—back when she was urging me to write a book about all the dogs we've raised and loved. Here is her story of Tasha.

MOTHER'S STORY

When I was young, Mother would take me each year to the Westminster Dog Show in New York. My uncle worked for a company that supplied some of their employees with free tickets, and this was an annual event, a special mother-daughter occasion, always followed up with lunch in one of the local Chinese restaurants.

Amid the excitement and tension of fame and glory in the dog world, Westminster introduced me to dog show mania. Westminster was and still is one of the few dog shows in the United States where spectators can touch some of the most winsome dogs. The hopeful canines wait on benches separated by a petition between each dog. We could talk with the owners, who were always ready to discuss the merits of their breed.

At one of those shows, I fell in love with Samoyeds. Could there be a more magnificent dog? Their snow-white coat, glistening with silver tips, eyes rimmed in black, and smiling dark lips sent me to the moon and back. I vowed one day I'd have my very own Sammy.

Years later, my husband was involved in starting a new business, and I needed a hobby that would keep me involved and uncomplaining about his lack of family time. The opportunity arose, and I did what in the dog world is an unforgivable deed. I purchased through the newspaper a Sammy from a backyard breeder. While many small-time breeders are reliable and take the necessary steps to provide healthy dogs, some don't. Too many people have purchased dogs through puppy mills that don't adequately protect the pet with shots and deworming, and then the unfortunate animal becomes a burden to his new owner.

However, our breeder was not one of them, and after seeing this knockout Sammy female, I knew she'd be going home with us. The breeder handed me her AKC registration papers showing her pedigree, and as my eyes scanned the names of my new dog's ancestors, I noticed many names written in red ink. The breeder explained that those were the champions that had produced the latest member of our family.

Fond memories returned of my trips to Westminster, and I asked if there was anything about my new Sammy that would prevent her from being shown. I didn't think about winning, but I imagined how much fun it would be to compete. We named her Tasha, and I decided that she would become a show dog.

Little did I know that this white bundle of fur would take our family for the next twenty-three years into the world of dog shows from inside-the-show ring.

We arrived home with Tasha in November, and her training began. She would be just the right age for the puppy class at the April Atlanta Dog Show.

We started going to training sessions to prepare, and Tasha proved to be a quick learner. She loved the treats that kept her standing at attention while I recruited a friend's child to look at her teeth, rub their hands down her back, and generally give her a good once-over. I decided my oldest daughter would show her, and we would see how it went.

The winter months flew by, and April arrived. While Tasha quickly learned the fine etiquette of dog obedience in the show ring, she also enjoyed being a care-free puppy. Digging holes in the red Georgia clay and creating moonscapes of inverted mountains kept her busy.

Soon our beautiful snow-white show dog was the color of red Georgia clay, and the show was only days away. How could I, with my limited knowledge, turn her red-stained coat into the fresh, fluffy white coat of the Samoyeds at Westminster? Since I'd gone to many shows, I knew how to present a dog, but I did not know how to groom that Eskimo coat.

After a few calls, I found a lady groomer in the Atlanta area who assured me that Tasha's white coat would sparkle under her care. Little did I know the lady was a professional dog handler who later became a respected dog show judge.

A few years later, I sold her a dog she would handle from puppy to championship. Just as promised, Tasha's coat became virgin snow-white once again. All we had to do was keep her that way for a few days.

The annual Atlanta Dog Show extravaganza took place at the Budweiser facility south of downtown Atlanta. The weather could not have been better, and the show site was splendid. We entered Tasha in the Bitch 6 to 9-month puppy class.

My oldest daughter did a masterful job of dog handling, and nobody could have guessed it was their first time in the ring together. The blue first place ribbon was a given, as Tasha was the only one in her class.

That was the first of many blue ribbons over the next two years. With four three-point majors and a few minor points, Tasha earned the fifteen points necessary to be given the coveted championship title before her name.

Tasha was not a natural show dog. She was moody and would've preferred to spend her days in the backyard digging her perfectly symmetrical deep holes. One would have thought she'd gone to hole-digging school. We'd look out the window into the backyard and see Tasha's fluffy white tail swishing through the air as she dug another hole to China. Once satisfied with its size and shape, she would crawl in it and spend the better part of the day enjoying her latest endeavor.

One Easter, we decided the time had come to fill in her holes and update the backyard moonscape. We arrived home from Sears with fifteen large rhododendron bushes. After planting, we were ready for the extended family to join us for Easter dinner and show off our renovated yard.

Early the next morning, our neighbor called and told us to look out back. I was shocked to see Tasha had dug up all the bushes, pulled them out of their holes, and placed them end-to-end on our circular driveway.

We made one more attempt to plant the now wilted rhododendrons, but our champion Sammy did the same thing again. The backyard was her moonscape with all its doggy holes, and no bush invaders would fill up her manicured works of art. We lived there for ten more years and never planted another bush.

Tasha was our first Samoyed, but not the last. The years passed, and many more Sammies lived with us. Not one ever dug a hole.

SAMOYED

Gypsy was not a Samoyed, but in some ways, she looked like one. She was smaller-boned and more fragile in stature, less muscular, and her ears flopped over in contrast to a Samoyed's pointed ears. But she had medium length white fur that is reminiscent of the breed. Perhaps a Japanese Spitz would be a better comparison. If DNA testing were available back then, it would have been interesting to know her origins.

Soon I learned all about Samoyeds. I'd never heard the word before —who invented such an unusual name? Spelling was never my forte, so out of curiosity, I looked the word up and chuckled. There is more to the name of the breed than one might imagine.

The common Russian etymology of the name "Samoyed" means "self-eater." In other words, cannibal—people eating people. Perhaps because they lived in such a hostile world reaching up into the Arctic, the native people were the subject of much folklore.

Another more probable linguistic translation is from the Sámi nomadic tribe, which means "land of the people." These ancient land dwellers have occupied the northwest reaches of Russia for centuries. The landmass is known locally as the Murmansk Oblast.[1]

As I dug a little deeper, I discovered the Sámi people speak several dialects. The most widely spoken is Northern Sámi. My curiosity took me a little further. Had the Bible been translated into this ancient language?

I discovered that the Evangelical Lutheran Church of Finland (ELCF) finished the full Bible translation of the Northern Sámi language in 2019. The translators hope it will strengthen the cultural identity of these nomads as they are the only indigenous people in Europe. About 15,000 to 25,000 native speakers remain. In the words of Sámi theologian Helga West: "Now I understand many Bible passages in a new way as they rose from my own cultural context. Only now does the Bible speak also to me."[2]

While I find all of this fascinating now, back then, my focus was more personal. I remember sitting at the breakfast table one morning and seeing Tasha running around in the backyard.

I loved seeing a white furry dog out there with Gretchen, but I was sad it wasn't Gypsy. Everyone else seemed to have moved on. I hadn't. But at least Gretchen had a four-legged friend to play with again.

DOD SHOWS

Before I knew it, we were going to dog show training sessions in Buckhead, an Atlanta suburb forty minutes away, every Thursday night. I soon discovered as novices and experts arrived with canines of all shapes and sizes how little I knew about dogs. My sister at seven could identify more breeds than I could.

One of the first competitions we entered, sponsored by the American Kennel Club, was in Augusta, Georgia. Little did I know that only a few years later, I would move to this town when my ex-husband enrolled at the Medical College of Georgia.

Since I was only an amateur from a few training classes, I didn't have a clue what I was doing on the big stage, but Tasha won her class, and mom was hooked. Because of Mom's enthusiasm, eventually she got everyone else hooked, too. Soon we were traveling all over the Southeast entering dog shows, from Birmingham to Ashville to Spartanburg to Chattanooga, but there was a problem. We only had one dog, and my mother and I both wanted to be the handler.

The Atlanta Dog Show was a turning point. My mother and I had a spat trying to set up a tent. Neither of us knew what we were doing, and we blamed each other for our total incompetence. After well over an hour, the tent lay on the ground, and we weren't speaking. Where were my brother and Dad? They could have put this tent up in seconds. I guess I should have been a Girl Scout.

After that debacle, I lost interest in being a handler. At sixteen, I had other things on my mind. My sister was eight, the perfect age for junior handlers, and she was terrific at it. My mother and sister became the dog show fanatics. They would spend hours discussing the finer things of dog finesse—the best bait, the best judges, the best breeders, and on and on.

I missed Gypsy, and while I was glad everyone else had chosen this path to heal, it didn't assuage my grief in the same way. I eventually parked myself in front of the obedience ring as everyone else hung out by the show ring.

I admired the outstanding skills of obedience dogs. They weren't just competing in a beauty contest that was skin deep. They had to exhibit skills in various areas that relied on their brains, noses, eyes, and ears. To achieve that level of skill required commitment and teamwork between the dog and the handler—nothing short of a beauty to behold. To this day, I remember one Sheltie that was outstanding, and that dog took the prize.

I enjoyed all the excitement surrounding the dog shows. It transformed the family and brought us together. Mother became a breeder, and over the next few years, she added more dogs to the family. Dad purchased a bus in which to transport multiple dogs to the competitions.

Eventually, my mother and sister finished five champions—quite a feat considering most of those dogs they bred and raised. One year Mom and Dad were the directors of the high-profile Atlanta Kennel Club Dog Show.

Mom and Dad had always enjoyed collecting antiques, and soon they began to collect dog figurines. Dad would find some obscure piece for Mom and give it to her for Christmas or her birthday.

Sometimes I would go with Dad when he would pick it out. I loved seeing the twinkle in his eye when he found something rare. Soon there were dog figurines all over the house. I still have a few of them, all these years later.

After a while, my brother got involved in junior handling. Soon he was showing a bulldog. What a strange dog, but my brother looked quite spiffy dressed up in a suit. Maybe there was hope for him. He was quite handsome when he wasn't dirty.

While winning was always exciting, memories with my family are what I treasure most today; the laughter, the food, and the camaraderie. I'm glad I went to as many dog shows as I did and wish I'd gone to more.

By that time, my life was about boys and looking forward to college. While I longed to be on my own, I hated leaving my brother, sister, and aging German Shepherd. My parents—I was okay with leaving them.

One of my fondest memories is when I showed up unannounced at a dog competition in Montgomery, Alabama, for Mother's Day. I was dating my ex-husband, and we surprised Mom by driving from Athens, Georgia, to Montgomery, Alabama. I'll never forget her shocked face when I walked up to her as she groomed her Sammy. I handed her a big bouquet and wished her Happy Mother's Day. She broke down and cried.

After Gypsy died, Gretchen was my favorite dog. The Samoyeds with their championship pedigrees had overshadowed Gretchen, and I got left behind in the dog world when I quit showing. I barely knew the names of the Samoyeds. Besides that, big dogs don't live as long as smaller ones. Without a car, my trips home on the bus were infrequent, and I hated to think Gretchen would grow old while I was an hour and a half away.

When I did come home, I made it a point to spend time with Gretchen. When I walked through the front door, she'd be lying on the kitchen floor built for one cook flapping her tail on the floor and wet kisses soon would cover my cheek.

The summer following my freshman year is one I'd like to forget. I couldn't figure out what I wanted to do career-wise, and Mom and Dad insisted I graduate with a degree that would earn me a well-paying job. We reached an impasse, and I didn't return to The University. Instead, I enrolled at Brown College of Court Reporting, but I never gave up on my dream to return to college.

Noah

Despite the turmoil that summer, I have one favorite memory of toying with the champion dog, Noah. He belonged to my sister. We had relocated the family business out of the house to an office building my senior year in high school. So the summer after I returned from The University of Georgia, my fiancé and I would hang out in the newly renovated basement where we crated the dogs.

One night we made Noah go in and out of the crate several times to tease him. Even though he wanted to sleep, he complied graciously with our teenage angst. Back when there were no cellphones, computers, internet, Netflix, HBO, and all the forms of entertainment we have today, we had to make our own, so we "played" with the dog.

Ecclesiastes in the Bible says there is a time for everything under the sun. The one good thing about living at home again was I could baby Gretchen in her senior years. I still longed for the white dog that came to me in a thunderstorm, but I loved Gretchen. She would lie beside me when I sang and played the guitar on the back porch. She was not as agile as she once was, suffering from hip dysplasia common in larger dogs, so she was content to listen to me serenade her.

Gretchen was my last link to childhood. That link broke the day I said goodbye to her. I went home and cried in the arms of my ex-husband. We had recently married, and a few months later, another dog mysteriously appeared on our back porch—just like Gypsy a decade earlier.

9
SHELLEY

Shelly

I didn't realize how much I'd miss having a dog when I married. My sister's gerbil gave birth to babies, and so we adopted one of them. My sister told me what I needed to do to make the rodent happy, and I bought a large fish-tank for the brown furry critter and lots of gerbil extras. I didn't know you could spend so much money on a rodent. Despite being fun to play with in between dictating court reporting notes, she wasn't quite the same as a dog.

Our new abode was quite plain, but the hundred-year-old house was perfect for newlyweds. I always had a penchant for old homes with high ceilings, wide hallways, and front porches that never get used. A long foyer split the house down the middle. We even had a mail slot. That's a big deal when you're newlyweds.

I'd found the ad for the rental in the *Atlanta Constitution* a few months before we married, and my ex-husband moved in and fixed it up. The house was on a major road in downtown Atlanta, only a few blocks from Georgia Tech, where my ex-husband had transferred when I enrolled in court reporting school.

Even back in the 1970s, $80 per month was a ridiculously low price. The owner was a retired carpenter and had converted part of his house into a small apartment rental. The couple were well into their eighties and lived on the other side of the house.

The house apartment came fully furnished. A small dining table and two chairs faced the sofa in front of a window, and the refrigerator was right next to the sofa. We had just enough room to walk between the couch and the table. An old floor heater was on the short wall between the hallway and the bathroom, and we squeezed a television in the small space next to it.

The owner had added the bathroom as a separate addition. We didn't have a shower, but we had a bathtub with little feet. We bought a blue rug to cover up the brown painted concrete floor in the bedroom, and my ex-husband carved up a bathroom rug to conceal the old-style tile in the bathroom.

We were two lovebirds, and the only extra expense we invested in was an air conditioning window unit for the bedroom. The elderly couple couldn't have been better landlords, so we left the air conditioning unit behind when we moved out a year and a half later.

One night we cooked hamburgers on a tiny grill outside of our tiny apartment. The next morning, my ex-husband saw a small black and white Basenji-looking dog licking our grill and called me to come see her. I was getting ready to go to work as I had just taken a job as a court reporter for a firm in downtown Atlanta, but I hurried into the living room.

My heart did somersaults when I spotted the small dog, but she was too cute not to belong to someone. Questions filled my mind. We lived on one of the busiest streets in Atlanta, and cars zoomed by twenty-four hours a day.

Fearing she might run away, I opened the front door and coaxed her inside. She dashed into my arms, and I picked her up and held her as she licked my face. I was smitten with love and wanted to keep her. She seemed to me to still be a puppy, or she was just a very small dog. For sure, she was too fragile to survive as a stray. Maybe she had just been weaned from her mother.

I had to go to work, so we couldn't decide what we should do right then. When I returned that evening, my ex-husband had been home all day and said no one had come by looking for a missing dog.

Our carpenter landlord was already building an outdoor fenced-in play area, complete with a doghouse, and he had put up a heavy-duty wire similar to what Dad had made for Gypsy. Even though chained, Shelley, our new dog, could still run and fetch a ball.

Did God bring Shelley to me? It seemed too good to be true. However, I needed to make sure she wasn't someone's pet. Holding her in my arms, we walked down the street, knocking on doors. No one recognized her or knew to whom she belonged, so I claimed her.

We took Shelley to the vet to have her checked out and spayed. I knew how much work puppies were, and we didn't want that responsibility.

I asked the vet, "What kind of dog is she?"

"Probably a Basenji mix," he replied. "Has she barked?"

I shook my head. "Do Basenjis bark?"

"They have a different kind of bark," he said, "more like a b-a-r-o-o."

What kind of bark was that? Gypsy, Gretchen, and the Samoyeds just had a typical bark.

I remember the first time I heard her bark. We'd had her for a few months, and it wasn't the typical dog sound. In fact, I laughed at the silly imitation, as if she was trying to bark but didn't know how. She made a loud yodel, long and barooing, or one long b-a-r-o-o.

I was happy to hear her b-a-r-o-o. Whoever heard of a dog that can't yelp? And she also made other affectionate sounds that I would describe as her unique form of talking. I enjoyed her sweet dog noises when she was excited, and I learned to ignore her howls when she was jealous of me talking to someone. She was like a spoiled child. She didn't want to share me with anyone.

I never thought I could love another dog as much as Gypsy, but Shelley came close. God must have known I needed Shelley, much like I needed Gypsy.

I was thrilled when my ex-husband got accepted into medical school on his second attempt, and the grand day arrived when we packed up our things and moved. I couldn't wait to set my four-legged black and white baby loose in the grassy backyard of our new home in Augusta, Georgia. She had never been able to run around unattached to a chain, and I even had a job waiting for me with the same firm.

10
FIFI

Fifi

After we pulled into the driveway of our red brick home for the next four years—our very first house—my heart raced with anticipation. There was even an overgrown garden at the very back if I wanted to do some gardening.

However, it contained row after row of some kind of ugly plant I'd never seen. When I asked the realtor what they were, she said, "The owner loves artichokes." To me, they looked like weeds. The name alone was enough to deter me from wanting to try one.

The backyard abutted an easement, so there were no houses behind us. On the other side of the easement was a major highway. At night before drifting off to sleep, I'd hear the truckers zooming down the road.

I excitedly removed Shelley's leash and watched as she studied the fenced-in backyard. Once she realized she was free, she took off racing in circles as fast as her little legs would move. She'd always been on a chain, but now she could run all she wanted.

Soon after we moved in, we put in an alarm system. It was a good thing because somebody tried to steal our canoe and boat. I'd bought both as gifts for my husband. The would-be thief triggered the alarm. The company called me at work and notified the police. I'm sure the loud siren scared the bejesus out of the robber. Luckily, he wasn't interested in a little black and white, short-haired mutt.

When I came home, I found the canoe sitting in the middle of the yard where the robber had dropped it. No doubt, he hopped over the fence and headed for the highway. I worried he might come back. If only dogs could talk.

Shelley preferred being outside during the day when I went off to report depositions that were—well, let's say that litigation in the boonies is not as diverse or interesting as litigation in the metropolis of Atlanta. The cases mostly involved discrimination, workers' comp, construction issues at Plant Vogtle—I was afraid that place might someday explode—malpractice lawsuits, and Ft. Gordon Army personnel issues.

For the first time since I began working as a court reporter, I came home smelling like cigarettes. Between the smoke from attorneys and the pollution from billowing stacks around Augusta's manufacturing plants, I had to take allergy shots to deal with sinus issues. The environmental movement was years away, and the air quality some days, depending on the wind, was putrid.

When my allergies were super bad, I'd be so hoarse I had a hard time dictating my steno notes into the old Dictaphone unit. Shelley would lie on the floor beside my desk, listening to my voice drone on and on, until I got so hoarse she would leave.

"Enough is enough," is what I imagined her saying.

Thank goodness those days ended. They were not the glory days of court reporting. That didn't happen until computers could automatically translate those steno notes into English, paving the way for closed captioning.

If you've never lived in the Deep South, you may not want to. It's a different planet. Atlanta is NOT the Deep South.

Back then, attorneys in the boonies smoked cigars like they were God's gift to humanity. And Blacks (they weren't yet called African-Americans) spoke a different dialect of English. I made up plenty of answers to questions posed by attorneys. I could only ask witnesses to repeat their answers a few times before they'd look at me with contempt, and the attorneys would roll their eyes. We didn't use tape recorders, although I should have. It would have made court reporting less stressful.

I don't think those chauvinistic lawyers in Augusta liked me. I sure didn't like them, but maybe all that inability to understand the Southern dialect helped me with my creative writing. Nobody ever complained about a transcript, so I guess I did a pretty good job of inventing answers to stupid questions that only an attorney would ask.

Augusta was so discriminatory against women; did I say discriminatory? The attorneys were accustomed to a male court reporter handling their depositions, and they made me feel unappreciated and unwanted. I think they expected me to work for minimum wage. The Good Ole Boys Club of Augusta wasn't ready for an enterprising young woman from Atlanta, Georgia.

I was in tears when a prominent attorney railed about a bill on a demanding job, so much so I think my Atlanta boss feared I'd have a mental breakdown, so he spoke to one of the leading attorneys. He paid the bill in full and never abused me again. After all, I had to support my husband and feed a dog that thought she deserved steak dinner every night.

Once, we went to the airport to see all the rich and famous golfers depart when the Augusta National was over. We watched as Leer jets took off one after another. I didn't even know who'd won.

Right then I knew I should have gotten a degree in golf. Where was my brain on something as important as that? Of course, I'd tried golf once and managed to hit everything but the ball. The course was never the same after all the divots I carved out of their well-manicured landscape. My ex-husband left a big tip for the caddie.

One day we bought a rocking chair, and my grandmother said, "First comes the house, then comes the rocking chair, and then comes the baby." But Shelley was my baby. She was as possessive as an only child. When I'd have a long conversation with my mother or a friend on the telephone, I'd have to retreat to the bathroom or put her outside. She didn't want to share her "mother" with anybody.

When I would come home at night, Shelley would run around the house before plopping down on the couch. Then she'd wait for me to dote on her. Considering how much I hated court reporting in Augusta, Shelley was God's gift. I worked way too much overtime, but she faithfully kept me company day after day.

When my ex-husband was on night rotations his junior year, I was thankful Shelley would yodel at any outside noise. Even though I knew she would never bite anyone, she would b-a-r-o-o, which was enough to scare away any potential prowlers.

One time we took Shelley for a ride in the canoe the thief tried to steal. She was usually compliant and never did anything stupid—except when we took her on that trip. Unexpectedly, she jumped out into the cold water. She must have seen a fish. We had her on a leash, but she didn't have on a life preserver.

I tried to pull her up as she struggled to stay afloat, but all I did was choke her. She was a complete wreck, only slightly more than me. Eventually, my-husband jumped into the cold water to retrieve her. They both had blue lips and chattering teeth all the way home. That was the end of Shelley's canoeing days.

We didn't dare risk taking her out in our ski boat to the Clark Hill Reservoir. But Shelley didn't care. She was a homebody chasing squirrels and b-a-r-o-o-i-n-g at anything that moved in her territorial backyard.

One winter, it snowed, and she fetched the snowballs we made and ate them. As small as she was, she wasn't afraid of anything. She had an excellent opinion of herself and had no problem telling me.

On my way into work one morning, a long line of cars was backed up on Greene Street. Brown Court Reporting, Inc., was several blocks farther. Bored, people had turned off their engines and were waiting.

I exited my car and walked up the street. "What's going on?" I asked some people hanging around.

A man said casually, "Apparently, a dog got hit by a car."

My heart welled up as I wondered how badly the dog was hurt, who he belonged to, and if he would be okay, but the man didn't know anything more.

I waited a few more minutes. When it didn't look as though things would clear out anytime soon, I turned around and went a different way to work.

Throughout the morning, however, I thought about the little dog hit by a car. I wanted to know more. I left the office and started checking with some of the businesses on Greene Street. Did anybody know what happened? "Somebody transported the dog to a local veterinarian," someone said. I scoured around. I found the vet and called to inquire.

"No," the lady said on the other end. "We haven't located the owner, but she needs immediate medical attention. Her leg is severely injured and requires amputation."

"How much is that?" I asked.

"About $200," the woman replied.

That was a lot of money back in those days, but now that I had involved myself this much, how could I not help?

I told her. "I'll pay the $200 if she'll live."

"Are you sure?" she asked. "It's not your dog."

I was sure. My only worry was how I would explain everything to my ex-husband. He wouldn't want another dog. I wasn't even sure if she and Shelley would get along. Shelley had never had to share us.

"When can I come by and meet her?" I asked.

"Why don't you wait till later this afternoon after the surgery."

I spent the rest of the day concocting a story to tell my ex-husband

—that I had rescued a dog from certain death, the dog was an amputee, and I'd paid $200 for surgery on a dog I'd never seen.

Finally, the veterinarian's office called and said the surgery was successful. I could come to see her, but they wanted her to remain overnight until she was well enough for me to take her home.

"Have you heard from anybody claiming to be her owner?" I asked.

"No," she said. "We don't know who she belongs to."

Later that afternoon, I dropped by the animal hospital. They were glad to meet me. I gave them the check for $200 and thanked them.

"Do you want to see her?" the tech asked. "She's in recovery."

"That would be great," I said.

They took me to an adjoining room, and I poked my head in the door. In front of me was a scrawny-looking, tan-and-white Terrier. She had large, floppy ears, and strands of hair covered her closed eyelids. Fifi aptly described her—a hurt, orphaned dog in need of a forever home. She lay curled up in a little ball with one huge bandage where her right hind leg used to be.

I left the vet's office with mixed emotions. I was glad I saved her life and could give her a home, but how would I explain it to my ex-husband?

"You did what?" he asked when I was halfway through my prepared speech.

I justified everything, saying we would find a home for Fifi, and I didn't plan on keeping her. Of course, he knew me better than that. By the time we went to bed that night, he had given a half-hearted yes to the new addition to the family, provided Fifi and Shelley got along. I was more than willing to make sure of that.

Two days passed. We brought Fifi home and slowly introduced her to Shelley. At night, we crated her. Fifi was still wearing a wrap where her leg used to be and still getting used to having only three legs. After a few days, we settled into a routine. I was encouraged that things were working out. Even my ex-husband quit complaining about the extra work.

A couple of nights later, the veterinarian's office called me. "We wanted to ask you a personal question."

I wasn't sure where this was going. "Sure."

"We wanted to know how things were working out with Fifi."

"They are working out fine," I said. "Fifi is getting along well with Shelley. Why do you ask? Did you find the owner?" I didn't want to know.

"Oh, no," she said. "It's just that we had a client in today with his sick dog that passed away. We couldn't do anything for him. In a strange coincidence, Fifi looked like his dog. The old man is heartbroken," she went on, "and we thought if things hadn't worked out, maybe you would be willing to let him adopt Fifi."

"We could meet and see what happens." After I hung up the phone, I wondered if she had told the man that Fifi only had three legs. Not everybody would want a three-legged animal.

He called me the next day, and I promised to come home early to meet him. By this time, I wasn't sure I could let Fifi go. She had become a part of our family.

I arrived home, and a short while later, a car pulled up in the driveway. I walked outside to greet the man. As he exited the car, I noticed something odd that caused me to do a double take. He had a cane. He put the walking stick out to steady himself and then dragged his bad leg behind him. The man was disabled.

Then I realized, I was only the keeper of Fifi until her new master picked her up—someone who could understand what it was like to have three legs. As the older man and Fifi left, God reassured me that her new home would be perfect. I learned later the vet donated the $200 I paid to help another dog in the future.

After four years of living in the Augusta hellhole that golfers think is heaven, I wanted to get on with life. That day couldn't come soon enough, and we moved to Gainesville, Florida. It didn't take twenty-four hours for me to think I'd died and gone to heaven. Of course, after four years in Augusta, any place would have seemed like heaven.

II

BUGS AND FURRY FELINES

When we moved to Gainesville in 1983, I decided to try my hand at gardening. I'd never had a garden, and I was clueless about how to make stuff grow. I figured all you had to do was throw some seeds in a hole, add a little water, and wait for the sun to make the seeds sprout. But nothing happened.

Where was the magic? Maybe I should have subscribed to *Southern Living* or gone to the library. There was a time when people did that. I think libraries now are just museums. Recently I went to one in Jacksonville, Florida, and I was sitting in a chair cross-legged enjoying a book. The librarian came up and scolded me, "You need to put your shoes on and put your feet on the floor."

So I left. I was going through cancer treatment and didn't want to be around a bossy, grumpy turd. I guess the librarian was bored because there were no other book lovers to badger about sitting etiquette. But I digress.

Back in 1983, I should have looked up the directions—how to plant seeds that grow—but I hated reading instructions. I enjoy fantasy more.

Maybe there was not enough sun or too much sun. Must have been the sandy soil. That was it.

No, it was those Florida bugs, those big, brown ones with antlers a mile long that fly inside when you open the door or a window Once, I had a cockroach that fell into the bathtub while I was bathing. Another time I was sleeping, and I felt one tickling my arm. I never opened the window again.

One time a large one crawled up my steno machine while I was captioning. And then there was a time I had one attack my leg when I was playing the piano. I even had one that fell on my head while I was reading a scary novel.

Those deplorable flying vermin ate my seedlings. That was it. There better not be any cockroaches in heaven, or God and I will have a long conversation.

Then I discovered the real culprit. Some trespassers were leaving their smelly, unwanted gifts in my garden. Little messes that cats sometimes cover and sometimes don't. One cat left his evidence. What was I to do? My neighbor had a white cat, a gray cat, a black cat, an orange cat—I can't remember any colors they didn't have.

How dare those furry felines poop in my garden! I wanted to walk two houses over and give my cat-keeping neighbor a piece of my mind. Their four-legged criminals were destroying my property.

I used to say that'd be the day when I'd get a cat. Our adopted stray dog, Shelley, hated cats more than I did. A short-haired, black and white Terrier mix that we rescued from the streets of downtown Atlanta, she was on cat patrol all day. A sweetheart she was—except when it came to cats.

I think I was just holding a grudge against cats. I'd still not heard one purr. The only sound I ever heard one make was when they howled or screeched, and they made it a point to do it when I was trying to sleep.

I gave up on my garden extravaganza, and a few years passed. More cats appeared. I only knew of one neighbor who had cats. How many did they have? One day I asked.

"We have seven."

Shaking my head, I walked away. How could anyone have that many? As it turned out, I was glad I never complained to them about their cats pooping in my garden. Several years later, when I began adopting cats, mine would poop in theirs. And one day, they politely told me my cats ate up the food they put out for their cats.

I told my furry friends to stay in my yard. Not that I didn't feed them. They just had big appetites. Maybe I should have fed them salmon. My cats never cared for chicken, but the chicken was cheaper than salmon.

12

BEACH TRIP WITH SHELLEY

The beach was always our favorite place, and Crescent Beach was close enough to drive over and back in a day. We didn't take Shelley to the beach often, but this day we included her.

We found a pristine, secluded spot, and we opened our umbrella. Shelley stretched out beside us, still on her leash, and I daydreamed underneath my hat that clumsily covered my eyes.

Overhead, a Man of War soared with graceful maneuvers, climbing ever so higher into the darkening sky. Make-believe rivulets followed behind him as in the wake from a boat. I watched for a long while until he was out of sight.

I relaxed beside my handsome rescuer from my younger days. While his sandy legs no longer had a mountain climber's physique, neither did I possess the physical beauty that captured him in a freshman chemistry class. Otherwise, I reasoned, he would treat me the way he once did.

"Do you love me?" I asked.

"Of course, I love you."

I turned my head again and stole another glance his way, realizing how rarely I saw his eyes without his thick-rimmed glasses. He had laid them on top of the Coke cooler under the umbrella. The assurance was only momentary, too fleeting. Why was it so hard for me to believe him?

Conceiving a baby seemed like a dream, beckoning me, taunting me. Everywhere I looked were children—other people's children. The elusive need to be not only a wife but a mother owned me.

We began with trips to the doctor to answer all those probing questions and submit to all the invasive intrusions every couple endures when nature can't seem to make it happen naturally. After following such a strict course of lovemaking, the spontaneity of the art had lost its passion. Conception had become my obsession and personal burden. There is nothing so lonely and disappointing than a barren womb that refuses to open.

I scooted closer, but not so close that our oily bodies from the thickly slathered suntan lotion touched. I knew if I asked again, he would respond with weariness. My questioning had become an obsession. I felt the gulf between us widening as my insecurity grew.

Changing the subject before his mood dampened the moment, I asked, "What would be your favorite boy's name?"

"Matthew would be a good one."

Of course, he knew I liked that name.

"Are you glad we came here?" I asked.

"What do you mean?"

"Are you glad we moved to Florida? You could have done your medical residency anywhere."

"I guess."

That was about as reflective as he ever got. Intellect and logic always took precedence over whimsical daydreaming. I wondered if he ever contemplated anything deeply. If something couldn't be added to, subtracted from, or put into a formula, he wouldn't waste time figuring it out.

However, in our college days, he was a romantic.

"If I could kiss the inside of you, I would," he told me when we were freshmen at The University of Georgia. That seemed like a millennia ago.

He first noticed me in chemistry class when he sat beside me and tried to woo me with silly words on his new calculator—the first wave of electronics that opened the world to modern technology. Computers were years away.

I was bored with his antics as I tried to focus on the professor and the meaning of such things as Boyle's law and molar conversions.

At eighteen, his legs would rival any bodybuilder or Olympian. He was the youngest to hike the Appalachian Trail the summer before, from Springer Mountain, Georgia, to Katahdin, Maine—all 2,175 miles through fourteen states.

Despite his good looks, gentle nature, and undeniable intelligence, he had yet to settle into academic life. His grades were a disgrace, and I told him so.

I feared what my parents would say if they knew the beau I was dating was on academic probation. However, when I threatened to drop him unless his grades improved, he made the Dean's List the final semester. His parents loved me.

After our freshman year at The University of Georgia, we packed our bags and dumped them into the back of his grandmother's '64 Rambler and headed south to Ana Maria Island, Florida. We spent the next week at his grandparents' home where they lived in "a house of everything turquoise" because his grandmother's favorite color was turquoise.

We were lovers in paradise as we splashed in the salty water, made sandcastles that baked in the sun, and strolled along the beach in the moonlight. He introduced me to beauty—heat lightening, fine wine, and ruggedness.

We stayed up until midnight each night to watch the night-blooming cereus open their white blossoms, and then we would be amazed at how quickly they withered. He treated me to the best restaurants. He made his dreams mine.

Two years later, we were back on the same beach when he proposed to me and slipped a beautiful diamond on my finger. I couldn't see it well in the darkness, but it didn't matter.

The only witnesses were the angelic stars in the sky and the tall ships on the sea. It should be mandatory that everybody fall in love before they die, just like teens can't get through the teenage years without zits. I hoped our love would last forever.

If only I could get pregnant. I had sacrificed my college dreams and then supported him after we married. Some marriages didn't survive medical school. I felt terrible for the wives who started with us but didn't make it to graduation. Of the ones who did, they had all been rewarded with babies—except me.

The tide was coming in, and the ripples of waves drew nearer to the towels beneath us. Soon we would have to move farther up from the shoreline if we didn't want everything washed away.

As fistfuls of water drew closer, I rested in the warmth of the coarse sand, digging in my heels and wiggling the grains between my toes. The salty air, the rippling tide, and the seagulls squawking amongst themselves stayed the same. Something was comforting in that sameness each time we visited the beach. The preoccupations that held me captive could be forgotten, and frustrations washed away, if only momentarily, by the pounding waves.

I sat up and realized the waves were almost touching us. "We need to move our stuff."

Shelley yawned and stretched, anticipating our relocation. As a surrogate child, she did her best to fill the mothering need within me. She made the wait for children bearable, although I don't know if it ever was bearable.

The sun was lower now on its daily trek across the ocean. I loved to watch it in the final seconds as it kissed the sea and disappeared.

A family closer to the shoreline was already taking down their umbrella as the tide encroached. The Asian couple's two little girls had built a giant sandcastle complete with moats and waterways that had succumbed to the rising water. Soon there would be no evidence left of their afternoon's work. Tomorrow the sand would be renewed to its pristine state as the tide receded, and the process would start all over again.

What would it be like to be their mother, read to them at night, tuck them into bed, play dolls with them, and dry their tears? I tried to imagine, but the dream always dissipated, like when one awakens in the morning trying to recall something from a dream the night before.

My ex-husband grabbed his glasses and stood. "I think I'll take Shelley for a walk up the beach. Do you want to go with us?"

I was in one of my reflective moods. "No, I'll wait here and watch you."

Shelley was ready for a pleasure jaunt along the water's edge. She patiently waited, wagging her tail, and getting tangled up in her leash as we brushed off the sand.

My ex-husband was the only man I'd ever loved. I'd gone through my share of boyfriends and had my pick of young beaus. I could always get a date in high school and college. The truth was, I would have been content to stay home and read or play the guitar on Friday nights, but my parents, convinced I was a social underachiever, enrolled me in modeling school.

My companions took off toward the water. I rested. Part of me longed to go, but I wanted to finish my thoughts. The sun was even lower as the rays of filtered light fell on the ocean. The redness of the sunset seemed otherworldly. Maybe I'd read too much science fiction. A seagull crossed the sky, creating a silhouette of black beneath the magenta red.

I grabbed our sandy belongings and scooted them several more feet from the tide's reclamation of the sand. Sitting back down on the wet, sandy towels, I hugged my legs and watched.

Shelley tugged on her leash toward the shoreline, running back and forth. I remembered how we first thought she was part Besenji because she never barked. Then one weekend, we boarded her, and our once quiet dog came home with a renewed zeal to exercise her vocal cords. Now she bellowed at the water, frolicking at the shoreline, pretending to chase fish that she was too dumb to catch.

The air was becoming nippy, and a breeze picked up, intimating a storm brewing. We would need to leave soon. Florida storms had a way of building up quickly and dropping buckets of unexpected raindrops. But before the storm burst, I would receive a life-changing vision.

13

THE VISION

As ominous storm clouds gathered overhead, I stood and walked down the shore to see if they were headed back. It looked like they had turned around.

The wind kicked up the sand, and I picked up the towels, shaking off the excess sand and draping them over my shoulder. I swished my feet through the water one last time. If the rain came before they got back, I would dash for the car.

My attention returned to my ex-husband and Shelley as they approached, but something was different. I rubbed my eyes. When I focused, I saw other shadowy forms. I blinked several times. As the figures became clearer, I could no longer see Shelley beside my ex-husband. Instead, I saw a woman and two young girls.

I wiped my face with the sandy towel, thinking I must be imagining things. Now the sand stung my eyes. I pulled back my disheveled hair from my face and tried harder to focus. I saw a laughing woman with dark, curly hair.

He turned and said something to her. They ran in slow motion as if I were watching a romantic movie with cinematic visual effects on steroids. Her black hair flowed behind her sensuously. She was young and beautiful. The two children in the shadows were girls.

I stared, transfixed. I couldn't comprehend what I saw. Who was the woman? Was this the nightmare that tormented me, the dream without an ending? I couldn't bear to think that he would do such a thing, though fears increasingly afflicted me.

The brooding sky mimicked my emotions. The sun had slipped beneath the ocean, and the redness was a mere afterglow. A powerful wave shot up from the sea, splattering my legs, reminding me I was still alive.

My fears got the best of me. My ex-husband would never do that—would he? Questions filled my heart. Can the future be changed, or is it immutable? Is my destiny controlled by me or something else?

Still in a trance, I didn't realize they were back.

He headed toward the car. "We need to leave before the rain comes."

A musty scent filled the air that in saner times I would have associated with the rain. Was the smell her perfume? I needed to reset, return to reality, but I couldn't shake off the vision.

My ex-husband walked up to me. "Are you okay?"

"Yeah," I lied. I wasn't going to tell him what I saw, but I couldn't resist asking the dreaded question. "Do you love me?"

"Yes, I love you," he said tersely. "Why do you keep asking me that?" The cadence of his words was too familiar. I had asked the question too many times.

"I just want to make sure."

He seemed satisfied and proceeded to load the stuff into the trunk, adding too much sand in his haste because of the falling raindrops.

Still shaken by the vision, I couldn't resist. "You would never leave me, would you?"

He stopped. "Why do you keep asking me that? Haven't I answered that a thousand times before?"

He rarely raised his voice to me. An awkward silence followed. "Are you sure you're okay."

Was he just feeling guilty, or did I look like I had seen something? I tried to convince myself I saw a phantom.

He lowered the umbrella and hoisted it into the plastic container as rain droplets dripped down his thick-rimmed glasses. Shelley tugged from the leash on his arm.

"I'll take Shelley," I said.

The skies burst open as we shut the car doors. Neither of us said anything as the sharp words lingered between us. We pulled out of the parking lot with the windshield wipers struggling to keep up with the rainfall. As the wipers splashed carelessly, my thoughts mimicked the blades' motion, going back and forth, mindlessly out of control.

Deep down, I felt unloved. If I carried my ex-husband's child, he would love me again. I had postponed having children. Now thirty years old, my biological clock was ticking.

I missed those earlier years of our marriage when we rented that little apartment from the couple in their eighties. Why did the good ole days seem so good? They didn't seem that way at the time. I glanced at Shelley. She might be the only baby we ever had.

The sound of the rain was deafening, and it forced me to remain silent. The beauty of the day was lost. I thought about where our things had been in the sand, now washed away by the incoming tide. There would be no evidence we had even been there. If only the storm could wash away my memory. I should have gone on the walk with them.

14
I WANT TO SING

W... *vs. W...* was just one more item on the judge's busy docket. I'd been in a judge's chambers countless times as a court reporter, but this time was different.

"I took away her dreams," my ex-husband told the judge.

We sat across from each other, separated by a dark chasm. Rivers of sadness flowed through my soul. A friend who came with me for emotional support reached over and grabbed my hand. I fought to hold back tears.

The day seemed surreal. I walked into the courthouse as a married woman. Less than an hour later, I walked out as a single person with a different last name—Roberts, my maiden name. Why should I keep my married name if I was no longer his wife?

Memories tormented me.

"You can go back to school when I finish and get your degree," he promised before we married. "You can become that writer you've longed to be since you were young."

It never occurred to me I could go back to school sooner. Why didn't I enroll in college when we were in Augusta? But I needed to let go of the past and move on.

James 4:8 in the Bible says, "Draw near to God, and He will draw near to you" (ESV). And that is what I did. I never doubted God was with me through our year-long separation.

The hardest part was I had to postpone my college education and go back to work as a court reporter. However, I learned to set healthy boundaries and refused to work seven days a week.

While my divorce was tragic, I did not want that to be THE defining moment in my life. Soon I was playing the guitar again with the church praise band. They extended me a lot of grace to survive my inadequacies as a singer. When I get to heaven, I've told God I want to sing harmony, and I plan on singing pretty loud when I enter those pearly gates. "Hear me, God? I need your help not to sound like Barney Fife."

I thought if I bought a canary, the bird could teach me how to sing. The first morning, as I lay in bed, I heard a sweet melodic canary voice streaming in from the living room. A bright idea occurred to me. I'd get another canary, and then the two birds could serenade each together.

I drove to Tallahassee to purchase a female canary from a breeder. I didn't know if they would mate, but I thought with a female by his side, he would sing twice as loud.

However, the strangest thing happened. Once Tweetie Bird had his lovely soulmate, he never sang again. Someone told me, "Why should he? He has his girlfriend now."

Throughout the separation, I was surprised that my ex-husband showed no love for Shelley. He made several trips to retrieve various belongings, and not once did he stop to pet Shelley or even acknowledge her.

Shelley would follow him from room to room wagging her tail expectantly. We had rescued and raised her together for seven years, almost the entire time we were married. All Shelley wanted was a warm embrace or a reassuring pat on the head.

My ex-husband's change of heart toward Shelley was heartbreaking. How could he be so cold—icy cold? Shelley didn't understand.

Despite his betrayal of me, Shelley still loved him. Each time my ex-husband would leave, I'd hug my "baby" and reassure her everything would be fine. Dogs know when something is wrong. Maybe Shelley needed a four-legged friend.

15
REX

When my ex-husband left, dumping me for an older, overweight, flirtatious woman with no morals, I was determined to bring happiness into my life. I needed a fresh start, so I resurrected a long-forgotten hobby.

Eons and eons ago, when I was a teenager, I became acquainted with what I termed "dog show mania." If I were to write the definition of what that is, I would define it like this: being addicted to dog shows.

These "addicted humans" fall into two groups. Group one are the neurotic gossips. They go about spreading rumors, imagined or real, to inflate their egos and give themselves a perceived advantage over their competition. In sports, competitors call it trash talking.

My family didn't fall into the neurotic gossips. That was beneath them, though they did do their share of trading secrets—this judge likes this body type or head or…you name it. As much as the entry fees cost, you might as well learn all those secrets, which in the end aren't really secrets.

My family joined the prim-and-proper enthusiasts. The only requirement of the prim-and-proper enthusiasts is to learn the jargon describing the tiniest, minutest detail of a perfect Samoyed specimen, or any other breed of dog.

Whether neurotics or prim and proper, humans of all body types would scuttle around the ring with a purebred dog before a judge better labeled, "Lord of the Dogs."

I didn't really fit into either of those categories. I actually thought those purebred dog enthusiasts were a little insane. Instead, I became infatuated with dog obedience. My fondest memories are camping out at the obedience ring. I admired those high I.Q. dogs that performed in the American Kennel Club Obedience Trials. Superman couldn't have beaten them.

As "perfect" as Shelley was, designer-dog fanatics would label her somewhat disparagingly as a "loveable mutt." She just didn't fit the bill of an esteemed pedigree required for sanctioned dog shows. In my biased opinion, though, I say mutts rule.

Nevertheless, Shetland Sheepdogs were often the top scorers in the obedience ring, and once my divorce was final, I began to date a young man from church who raised the perfect breed for obedience—Shetland Sheepdogs. I frequently visited him while one of his female dogs was pregnant, and once she delivered the puppies, I fell in love with a sweet little Sheltie.

My soon-to-be-dog Rex was a purebred with a champion pedigree to boot. With his excellent bloodline, I'd have one of the best breeds for obedience. I had it all figured out. At least I thought I did.

The day arrived. I brought Rex home with more fanfare than I wanted. As I drove down Newberry Road, a major Gainesville thoroughfare, Rex climbed out of his box on the front seat and tangled himself up in the seatbelt.

I drove faster because I didn't know what else to do. By sheer luck, a police officer spotted my sporty red Firebird zooming down the road. In the darkness, a swirling red and blue light filled my rearview mirror.

I looked for the best place to pull off, turned onto a side street, and parked. A stern voice bellowed through a blowhorn, "Exit the car."

I only had one problem. I couldn't get Rex untangled.

The police officer roared a second time, or was it a third? If I didn't get this figured out, I'd be headed to the brig. My blood pressure rose before I knew what that meant. At last, I was able to unclick the seatbelt and push open the door. Terrified, my new puppy buried his paws into my chest.

The officer shone his flashlight in my direction as he walked over. I think he was relieved I wasn't a bad guy. After all, I had the cutest Sheltie puppy in my arms. I began my sob story—"I was trying to get home quickly because my dog got out of the box …."

The police officer interrupted me. "Ma'am, go home, don't speed, and drive safely."

I nodded. Rex firmly secured, I got back in my red sports car and gingerly drove away. I made sure I kept my speed twenty miles below the speed limit, and my thoughts returned to what was most important.

How would Shelley react to Rex? Shelley didn't have all those champions in her mutt pedigree. Eight months after my ex-husband and I married, we found her eating leftover burgers on our charcoal grill in downtown Atlanta. She'd probably even gotten a few meals out of smelly garbage cans before she found our rack. Nope, she definitely didn't have a dog show pedigree.

I reflected back to my dog show days. How did those champion dogs in the dog show ring know they were hot stuff? They would strut around the ring pulling their handler in tow, sticking their nose up in the air and wagging their tail till it almost fell off. I'd been to enough dog shows to see all that fluff and haughty pompousness. I hoped Rex didn't let it go to his head like that.

Was I going crazy to become a dog-fanatic again? I must be regressing in I.Q. It was all my ex-husband's fault.

The truth be told, you have to meet precise specifications in the dog-ring, or you ain't show quality. No exceptions. Of course, the handler has to be an expert at baiting dogs—just like fisherman bait their fish.

For the uninitiated, the show dog has to stand motionless while a distinguished lord-of-the-ring judge looks at the head, the tail and everything in between. The judge might even rub his or her hand along the dog's back, step away and walk around him, or just stare at the dog for what seems like forever.

All the while, the dog isn't allowed to move. So if you want to win those coveted points, you have to figure out the best bait so your dog will stay posed until the "time out" comes when the judge has finished his thirty-minute assessment. Actually, it's not that long, but it sure seems like it when you've caught the eye of an attentive judge and you don't want your dog to move a tenth of an inch.

My mother discovered the best bait to keep her show dog posed was smelly liver. She would boil it on the stove and put the bait in little baggies to take to the show, but the smell lingered—for hours. I was not too fond of that putrid odor. Whatever I used, I wouldn't use cooked liver. Maybe steak, but not liver.

After I avoided the speeding ticket, I figured God was with me. We arrived home, and I carried my adorable puppy into the house. Shelley welcomed the new arrival better than I anticipated. I was reminded of the typical 1980s blockbuster movies that fizzled out with disappointing endings. The speeding ticket had more pizazz than their introduction.

As I'd hoped, Shelley was quite happy to have a doggie friend in the backyard when I was court reporting frivolous lawsuits. They quickly became close friends and she forgot all about my ex-husband. Rex was not only a great pal to Shelley, but he was faithful to her. He had better morals than my ex-husband. Let's just say at this point, my ex-husband was ex-history for both of us.

Rex and Shelley kept the yard spick-and-span of armadillos, turtles, raccoons, squirrels, and snakes. If one got stuck, I'd hear about it. They wouldn't quit barking, and that was my cue I needed to rescue some stupid animal, more than likely, a turtle.

Rex was a favorite of two middle school neighborhood girls. Not only was Rex handsome, but his obedience training made him a delight to walk. They would come over every week, and he loved the attention.

There was only one thing Rex didn't like. He didn't like being a show dog. He didn't like obedience training, he didn't like the show ring, and he would never be a top scorer. My hopeful champion wasn't into that riveting, jaw-dropping spectacle. Even crowd applause didn't perk him up. After several attempts to make him into something he didn't want to be, I gave up the dog shows.

To his credit, he placed a couple of times with third place ribbons. I proudly saved them in a keepsake book I can't find. The truth is, his happiness meant more to me than those ribbons. Instead of becoming a world-renowned show dog, he was content to be king of the backyard. His name Rex served him well. Shelley became his lovely queen.

When I decided I wasn't going to torture him with dog shows. I took him to the vet to have him fixed. The vet called me an hour later.

"We couldn't perform the procedure because Rex aspirated on the table. Did you feed him this morning?"

"No," I told the vet. "He hasn't had any food since last night."

I went to pick him up, and as the vet advised me, I stayed awake all night to make sure he didn't quit breathing. After that, I chose not to have his male equipment removed. Castration sounded too painful, anyway.

16
NO RECORD

A couple of years after my divorce, I learned about the External Degree Program at The University of Alabama. The University had a unique arrangement with the National Court Reporters Association to allow twenty-one college credits toward a bachelor's degree. That was almost a full year of college. It seemed too good to be true.

I jumped in my car and went to Santa Fe State College to get a copy of my transcript. Then reality set in when the office administrator handed me my academic record. I had thirteen A's and one F. Suppose that F should cause the rejection of my application?

I lamented. "If only I didn't have that F." I had re-enrolled at Santa Fe State College to retake the calculus class after dropping out of The University of Florida. But when we got to derivatives, I gave up. I couldn't concentrate, and it was hopeless to continue.

I summarized what happened to the administrator.

"Did you tell your professor?" the administrator asked.

I shook my head. "No."

He studied me for a moment. "Let me see what I can do."

I handed the sheet back to him, and he disappeared in a back office. I couldn't imagine that he could do anything.

The administrator returned a few minutes later, handing me the same yellow sheet of paper. I looked at the words written in large letters across the calculus class: NO RECORD.

I read it several times before it sunk in.

The administrator broke into my thoughts. "There is no record now that you ever took that class. It no longer exists."

I thanked him and left, tears flowing down my cheeks. As I walked through the parking lot to my car, I was convicted. I must forgive my ex-husband. Sobbing, I unlocked my door and scooted into the driver's seat. Dropping my head on the steering wheel, I prayed. I needed to extend the same grace to him that Santa Fe State College had extended to me.

If my ex-husband thought he took away my dreams at that court hearing, I would make sure he was mistaken. Jesus didn't want me to be a grudge holder. He wanted to give me something better.

A couple of years later, I began to date a nice Christian guy who lived a few hours away. I met him through a mutual friend. After a brief courtship, we got engaged. However, when his mutt met my dogs, Rex and Shelley, things didn't go so well, so I called off the engagement.

Well, not exactly, but it sounds good in a dog book. Rex could get along with any dog—just about. Shelley was the possessive one, but neither of my canines approved of his dog. After that, I decided God meant for my faithful dogs to be my lifelong companions.

17
GYPSY - NEVER GIVE UP

\

When The University of Alabama accepted me into the External Degree Program, I pursued my bachelor's degree with great gusto.

The External Degree Program was the only program of its kind in the United States and was patterned after the External Degree Program at The University of Oxford in England. The introductory class, which was a required course, helped students to understand what kind of learners they were. I discovered I was an experiential learner. That meant I learned best with hands-on experience, not sitting in a classroom listening to lecturers recite their notes.

I suppose that adventurous spirit was instilled in me by Gypsy as well as all the places I visited through books I read as a child. Arthur C. Clarke, Andre Norton, Isaac Asimov, and Ray Bradbury were among my favorite authors.

During that time, I had a summer membership at a local Knights of Columbus pool. One day, a group showed up to take scuba diving lessons. As I watched, it struck me: I can do this.

I had gone scuba diving on my high school graduation trip to the Virgin Islands. That turned out to be a disaster. My equipment was designed for a five-hundred-pound man, the face mask leaked at the corners, and I didn't know how to equalize the air pressure in my ears. As the happy divers took off for the deep, blue yonder, I was left behind to experience a disappointing, virtual dive.

But, as my childhood pet, Gypsy, taught me, don't ever give up.

I walked over to the dive master, asked for his business card, and within a few weeks, I enrolled in scuba diving classes. Forty hours later, I held an open water diving certificate in my hand. I went on to earn my advanced open water certificate and cavern certification. I wasted no time taking trips to all the springs in Florida, South Florida, the Caribbean, and dive destinations worldwide, including the Great Barrier Reef.

When I was scuba diving at the Turneffe Island in the Caribbean in August 1990, Saddam Hussein invaded Kuwait. We had no contact with the outside world, and while driving back to Gainesville, I stopped to get gas and saw the newspaper headlines.

The invasion by Hussein was significant. I was enrolled at the Institute of Holy Land Studies in Jerusalem for the following January. That was one of my last courses before graduation.

As the world focused on the Middle East and the U.S. debated whether to invade Iraq, I continued to make plans to go to Israel, despite much fear and trepidation from my parents and friends. Soon the day arrived. As I sat at the LaGuardia Airport on New Year's Eve, heaviness filled my heart. The El-Al personnel had interviewed and re-interviewed me about what I was planning on doing in Israel once I arrived.

When they called for boarding, they pulled me out of the queue and questioned me again. I produced everything I could to convince them I wasn't a terrorist. Or that I wasn't a mistress of a terrorist.

The reality was, I was not Jewish, I was traveling alone, I was young, and no tourists were going to Israel at that time. Only after much banter back and forth did they allow me on the plane, and I flew to Israel on January 1, 1991.

Upon arriving, I experienced a war zone first-hand. The Institute rounded up the students from the plane, and as we left the Tel-Aviv Airport and headed toward Jerusalem, nobody knew what was going to happen. It seemed surreal when I saw the green sign on the highway pointing toward Jerusalem.

18

"MUCH AFRAID"

My classes at The Institute of Holy Land Studies began on January 2, 1991. The timing of my arrival was volatile—right before the start of the Gulf War. Unrest and political gossip filled the city. A general strike was in progress in the Arab Quarter and East Quarter of the Old City, which only heightened the electrically-charged atmosphere.

The trip to Israel was educational, so the focus was on academics; specifically, the historical and geographical setting of the Bible. Blessed with rich cultural diversity and timeless tradition, Jerusalem is a mishmash of the old and the new. It's no surprise Jerusalem is known as the City of Stone with a mandatory stone facade on all of its buildings.

The first day we took a walking tour of the Old City. Hiking up and down the streets, in and out of bazaars, food shops, and tourist traps, our learning slowed to a comfortable, relaxing pace, which I very much appreciated because of jetlag. It's surprising what you notice in "slow motion."

The Jewish Quarter was beautiful due to the renovation work since the 1967 Gulf War. Particular attention was given to preserving the holy sites—in stark contrast to the Arab Quarter that was dirty and unkempt. The Arabs seemed to have little regard for Jewish history.

Due to a recent terrorist attack on the Temple Mount, tourists were not allowed. However, we visited the Western Wall at night, and the floodlights surrounding the two-thousand-year-old highly guarded historic site created an aura of mystique and sacredness. It's hard to put into words how it felt to be at the holiest spot in Judaic history, and a strong case could be made for Christianity.

Because of the political situation, the Institute staff kept a close eye on us. We weren't able to leave the Institute without an escort.

Throughout the day, the Muslim Call to Prayer filled the streets. Muslims pray five times a day. I didn't expect to see so many Arabs—I suppose more commonly referred to as Palestinians.

Just outside the Old City is the Kidron Valley, which is next to the Mount of Olives. While walking around with my small class of thirteen students, a little dog came up and started following us.

What was so unusual was the dog looked like Gypsy. She was white with a couple of brown spots, medium-long hair, and slight build. Her facial expression was Gypsy-like, and she wanted to be near me. She was so afraid she couldn't quit trembling.

I wanted to comfort her, pat her on the head, and reassure her, but she was too afraid. I had to keep up with the walking tour and focus on the professor, so I couldn't stay behind and befriend her. Still, I spent much time speaking kindly to her at the back of the tour group. I would have taken her home if I could. I thought about Rex and Shelley, how they had a warm bed to sleep in, and a home where they were safe.

Safety in Israel is tenuous at best. Jesus' words came to mind. He said in Matthew 23:37: "Jerusalem, Jerusalem, you who kill the prophets and stone those sent to you, how often I have longed to gather your children together as a hen gathers her chicks under her wings, and you were not willing" (NIV).

I was sad when we left the little dog behind to return to the Institute. All these years later, I've never forgotten her, the little dog that reminded me of Gypsy.

In retrospect, my trip to Israel was life-impacting. I never imagined

I would write six books of Christian fantasy that centered on Israel. Without that time in Israel, especially on the eve of a national crisis, I wouldn't have had the experience or background to write the *Seventh Dimension Series*. That little white dog I saw in the Kidron Valley is one of the series' main characters.

During the second week of the course, we took a bus trip to southern Israel. The three-day journey took us through some of the remotest regions in Israel. Our first stop was at the nature preserve at Zin Wadi. I fell in love with the ibex, the wild goats, as sure-footed on the cliffs as a gymnast is on a balance beam. The goats are native to the area, and mentioned in Psalm 104:18: "The high hills are for the wild goats."

I took some amazing photographs of these sure-footed animals jumping across the rocky terrain. God made the ibex for the high places, and in those high places, they find safety.

After leaving Zin Wadi, we went to Avdat, a historical site for the Nabateans, Romans, and Byzantines. The city was established in the third century B.C., located on the Incense Route, and was the second most important city after Petra for caravan traders.

After leaving Avdat, we stayed overnight at Mitzpe Ramon, located on the Ramon Crater. The terrain looked like a moon landscape with a long, deep crevice surrounded by spikes and rugged terrain splinters. As Israel's largest national park, it is also a nature preserve with an astonishing number of small desert creatures.

We passed through the Ramon Crater and down to the Wilderness of Paran. Here the Israelites spent the better part of their forty years wandering. Desolate and silent, the merciless sun blazed unrelentingly. Whatever wildlife there was in the area was hidden. We could have been on Mars, and it wouldn't have seemed more desolate.

We went through Ezion-Geber, where Solomon built ships for opening trade routes to Africa. Although there are no Biblical references to Solomon mining in the area, the copper mines were named after him.

After leaving Timna Park, we took the bus toward Eilat, Israel's southernmost city, a busy port, and a popular resort on the Red Sea's northern tip. Along the way, we stopped at a gem museum, where we saw how they excavated the mines' turquoise to make precious stones. Then we arrived in Eilat, and the tour guide had the bus driver drop me off at a scuba diving shop.

For a couple of hours, I felt like a princess. Maybe they thought I was. It was Friday, January 11, and Operation Desert Storm began on January 17, 1991. Most tourists had left the country since the war with Iraq was imminent. I was the only one suited up for a dive.

They outfitted me in a wetsuit, along with a B.C. and octopus. I had brought my mask and snorkel—and I followed the dive master outside. We walked around to the dive shop's waterfront, with air tanks on our backs, and waded out into the Red Sea.

Diving in the Red Sea was an event I'd hoped for but wasn't sure would happen. I'd never dove in a desert climate, and perhaps more than at any other time, I felt like I was in another world.

As we dipped below the surface, I was transported to the depths of imagination where everything above the surface was forgotten. I'd never had a personal tour guide before, and that only made the dive more enjoyable. I didn't have to worry about where I was or wonder where to go. The dive master knew all the best spots to see. He took me to an underwater eel garden, long, thin, green-like plants anchored to the bottom that pointed upward and swayed gently back and forth in the ocean current.

We saw a white ribbon eel, an octopus, sea cucumbers, and several poisonous lionfish. Following the spectacular adventure, the bus picked me up, and I returned to my classmates.

After visiting the Dead Sea, the lowest land area on earth, we got back on the bus to begin our ascent to Jerusalem. As we traveled, I could see the Dead Sea shoreline, and in the distance was a boatload of fishermen. Their fishing lines hung off the sides of the boat. What were they hoping to catch? There are no fish in the Dead Sea as the waters are ten times saltier than the ocean.

Solomon wrote in Ecclesiastes 11:1: "Cast your bread upon the waters, for you will find it after many days" (ESV). I don't think Solomon was referring to the Dead Sea.

During the three-day excursion, we were out of touch with the world. When we returned to the Institute, war seemed imminent. When the U.S. State Department asked non-essential American workers/visitors to leave Israel, I decided to evacuate, especially when the Institute pulled out the gas masks and syringes filled with an antidote to counter nerve gas.

I left the Institute in the middle of the night in a taxi full of other tourists in what could be described as a Hollywood made-for-television Great Escape. I was never so happy as I was that day when I arrived home to see the Statue of Liberty.

19
BARUCH

Baruch

A few months after I returned from Israel, I took a three-week trip to Australia and New Zealand with The University of Alabama External Degree Program. I supplemented the excursion with a three-day live-aboard dive off the Great Barrier Reef.

The spectacular reef covers 132,974 square miles, includes nine hundred islands, and contains almost three thousand individual reefs. When would I ever get another chance to dive off the largest reef in the world?

When I returned, Barnacle Busters, a local dive group, invited me to show my slides at one of the dive meetings. I wasn't that astute with an underwater camera, and this was in the days before photography went digital.

Nothing back then was automatic. My birth father was a professional photographer, and I imagined someday capturing the spiritual essence of "living photographs" as his work so aptly did. That requires skill and talent.

I can't say my underwater photographs were at that level, but the club was gracious and remarked about how awesome a couple of them were. If you take a hundred pictures, even an amateur can luck out on a few.

I supplemented my mediocre underwater slides with more spectacular slides of some of the places I visited, like the hot springs and geysers in Rotorua, New Zealand, and the Uluru-Kata Tjuta National Park in Australia. But the real story that night wasn't my slide presentation. I had a fortuitous cat encounter by divine appointment on the way home.

After the meeting, I drove home on Tower Road and got stuck at the red light before turning onto Newberry Road. When the light turned green, I made a right-hand turn and saw a kitten running across the road. Newberry Road has three lanes in each direction. I stopped my car, put it in park, jumped out, and ran over to the median as the kitten was starting to cross into the lane of oncoming traffic.

I raised my hands and waved to get the attention of the oncoming vehicles. Because it was dark, I couldn't be sure they saw me. The kitten was limping and wouldn't make it across the remaining three lanes.

Through the windshields, bewildered faces with popping eyes gawked at me. "Woman, are you crazy?" I imagined them saying. Yeah, I probably was. It's one of the boldest things I've done in my life. I ran out into the highway and grabbed the injured kitten. Then I held him up so the drivers could see him.

Shock spread across their faces. They had not seen him limping across the road. Now they understood. One of them nodded and gave me an encouraging smile. I jumped into my car, where there were now cars stacked up behind me. Someone honked because I'd stopped in the middle of the road. I ignored him.

My biggest concern was what I should do. Shelley would never let me keep him, and I had no idea how to take care of an injured kitten. However, I knew there was an emergency vet open at night. I had visited it once when Shelley ate some chocolate candy from my suitcase. So I took the kitten to the emergency vet and presented him for treatment.

The vet said he needed to stay overnight for observation. They were worried about infection as the wound was deep, although fortunately, his legs weren't broken. His injury could have been much worse.

I returned home, wondering what I was going to do. If I kept the kitten, Shelley would go insane. She was set in her ways at her advanced age and would never warm up to a feline.

The next day I went to pick up Baruch—as I had named him—from the emergency vet. He still needed special care, so I kept him in the bathroom over the next week. It would be an excellent way to see what Shelley would do, but once she discovered a cat behind the bathroom door, she was relentless to go in there. I feared Shelley might harm him.

As he improved over the next week, he purred. For the first time in my life, I heard and felt the sound of purring. I remembered the failed attempt with a cat when I was a child. That had been thirty years ago.

Baruch means blessed in Hebrew, and we had blessed each other. I saved his life, and in return, I received his love.

More than likely, he was a stray kitten from a stray cat living off the streets. He was black and white with soft fur and a sweet boy. He was the most adorable cat I had personally ever met, which was none, but that didn't matter. I had fallen in love with him. Now I had to figure out what I was going to do about my dog and cat problem.

Children love to imitate a dog's sound, but I've never heard a child imitate a purr. How do you even describe it? If you have never heard it, you can go to YouTube, search for cat purring, and dozens of videos will pop up. Cats even have different purrs. I've read that the most popular videos on YouTube are cat videos. Not dog videos, but cat videos. Who knew there were so many cat lovers?

If you aren't tech-savvy, I'll share that you can find just about anything on YouTube. For example, while working on one of my books, I researched what kinds of sounds you hear in Africa, and someone had posted a YouTube video about the roaring sands of Africa. I didn't believe it until I watched the video. So, if you want to hear a cat purr or sand roar, YouTube is the best place to go. I would know.

As I thought about what I was going to do, I remembered my neighbors who had too many cats, whose cats used to poop in my garden. Last time I checked, they had seven cats. If you have seven, what is one more?

Baruch and I visited my neighbors, and I shared Baruch's story, how I rescued him, and how I couldn't keep him because of Shelley. I wanted him to go to a good home, and if they adopted him, I could still see him as he grew up. Guess what? They kept him.

I remember the day I took him over after his injury healed. I was sad, but I knew my neighbors would take good care of him. He lived to a very ripe old age. I hoped God would send me another kitten or cat when the timing was right.

In the meantime, Shelley and Rex kept me busy. Shelley was twelve now, and Rex was four. My encounter with Baruch, as short as it was, was a window into the future.

20
MOTHER'S DAY, MAY 8 1994

Doctors diagnosed my dad—who adopted me when I was ten—with glioblastoma about a month after I received my bachelor's degree from The University of Alabama. Glioblastoma is a virulent form of brain cancer.

For the next fifteen months, I traveled back and forth between Gainesville, Florida, and Atlanta, Georgia, sometimes driving and sometimes flying, to spend as much time as possible with him. Following the surgery, which was not curative but palliative, I asked the doctor how much time he had.

The doctor replied, "About fifteen months."

True to his word, my dad lived for fifteen months. Half of all patients with the protocol Dad received live fifteen to sixteen months. Sadly, the survival rate hasn't changed much in the last twenty-five years.

Cancer or any other life-threatening illness changes our perspective on life. My grandfather, who I was close to, beat colon cancer twice. He would go on to outlive my dad by many years, until he was ninety-seven. As I've gotten older, I've come to realize how old that is.

At sixty-four, it's hard to imagine living that long. I've now outlived my father, and I thought he was old when he died at sixty-two. My memories of Dad in those last few months are precious.

I remember when Dad wanted a particular cereal from the grocery store, and he couldn't remember the brand name. He grabbed a pencil and paper and drew a picture of the box's cover in the minutest detail.

I immediately knew which cereal he wanted—Kellogg's Rice Krispies. To this day, the cereal box has the same front. How could he draw like that, yet not be able to speak? The brain is too complicated to understand.

Once, we had a conversation about the brain. Dad told me we only use a small portion of it. While that might be true, I soon discovered that what we do use is essential.

I saw his MRI before the surgery, and his neurosurgeon pointed out where the tumor was. Little tentacles spread out from the primary tumor, and they went everywhere, like a plant's roots. If only doctors could find a cure....

I grieved deeply over my father's illness. I was thrilled to finish my degree, but his disease tempered my joy. Life is like that—perhaps to remind us that our home here is only temporary.

As I spent time with my dad while he battled cancer, I couldn't help but think about how fleeting life is. I thought about the next decade and what that might hold. There was one thing I wanted more than anything. If I expected my dream to come true, I needed to make it happen.

After I broke off my engagement, I discovered becoming a mother was more important to me than getting married. I'd done more traveling than I ever imagined possible. I now had that degree that had eluded me for so many years. The grief from my divorce was in the distant past. As I faced losing my father, I prayed, "God, if it's your will, please give me a daughter."

I went to my prayer group and prayed about adopting as a single mother. It wasn't that common twenty-five years ago. I could have heard a pin drop when I announced it to my prayer warriors.

Their response was, "We'll pray about this."

They did pray, and two months later, after submitting my application, I brought home my three-year-old daughter from Nepal. I might have set the record for the world's fastest international adoption.

We arrived on Mother's Day, May 8, 1994. Gainesville, Florida, is a small airport, so we traveled from Los Angeles to Atlanta before coming to Gainesville. My mother, my best friend from Middle School, her husband, and their two children met us at the airport during our stopover.

I had hoped to see Dad also, but Mom didn't bring him. It had been over a year since his diagnosis and surgery. We knew his days were numbered, but my mother didn't want to talk about Dad. Instead, she wanted to meet her first granddaughter.

I learned later how much Dad had declined since I'd left for Nepal two weeks earlier. She didn't want me to be worried about him on my way home, especially on Mother's Day. God had performed a miracle, and we needed to celebrate.

Once again, tragedy amid joy, that's the world in which we live. I wrote a memoir, *Children of Dreams*, about the adoption of my two daughters. I won't go into details here except to mention one pertinent thing.

By mistake—or divine intervention—I packed a magazine for dog and cat supplies in my belongings. The catalog advertised everything dog and cat-related—dog food, cat food, dog toys, cat toys, dog bones, catnip, leashes, doghouses, dog crates, cat hotels, and dozens of weird things only a neurotic dog or cat lover would want.

When we were in Nepal, my daughter took great joy in emptying my suitcase, and when she did, she pulled out the catalog and flipped through the pages. She was more interested in that magazine than some of the other things I'd brought, like a toy telephone, playdoh, and picture books.

I noticed when we would leave the hotel and walk along the crowded, noisy streets of Kathmandu, she always looked for cats. She wasn't interested in dogs, only cats.

When she opened the catalog and turned the pages, she would search for the cat advertisements, and when she found one, she would point at the cat and chuckle.

I would say, "Meow."

It didn't take her long to figure out a cat said, "Meow." And pretty soon, she was imitating me. Guess what her first English word was?

When we arrived home, we didn't have a cat, but I was sure there was one waiting for us to adopt. Shelley was an old lady now at seventeen. I worried she might be jealous of my new daughter, but Rex had become a helpmate to Shelley and not just a playmate. Rex was always by her side. That reduced Shelley's constant need for my attention, and with a rambunctious three-year-old, Rex was a great "dog sitter."

Shelley lived two more years until she was nineteen. In all those years, she was never sick. The only thing Shelley ever needed was flea medicine for hot spots on her back.

Then one day, she quit eating. She would walk over to her food dish and lay down in front of it. I watched her lose interest in food and lose weight. At nineteen, she no longer ran around the house like a crazy dog, or interrupted my phone conversations, or chased squirrels in the backyard, or barked at the moon, or chewed on soup bones. She was tired.

The average lifespan of a dog is ten to thirteen years. Shelley outlived most dogs by almost a decade. I didn't grieve over Shelley like I thought I would. Instead, I was thankful I'd had her for so long—through my entire adult life, from twenty-two to forty-one. She went from being a stray on Atlanta's streets to becoming my companion during some of my toughest times. She was my baby until God made me a mother.

Will we see our animal friends in heaven? I wasn't sure back then, but I am sure now. I've saved the best for last.

21

MORE STORIES ABOUT REX

I loved being a mother. I loved every minute of it when my daughters were young. And I still do, even though now they are in their early to late twenties. When they were young, I dreaded that empty nest syndrome. I imagined them flying the coop, getting married, having kids, starting their own independent lives, and me being left all alone in a nursing home somewhere.

There is something in my nature that needs to be needed. Of course, I still have one daughter at home—when she's not on mission trips. And because she's switched majors a few times, she still has quite a bit of college left, but we won't talk about that.

However, even after being a single mother of two daughters, my love affair with dogs continued. Dogs need the security of a kind face, a helping hand, and reassurance that everything will be okay. Rex was the sole recipient of our love and affection when Shelley left us to chase squirrels over the rainbow bridge. In sixteen years, Rex was guilty of only one crime: getting into the garbage can.

One day I decided to do something about my garbage can woes. I couldn't count the number of times I'd come home to nasty leftovers strewn across the dining and living room carpet. He wasn't a picky eater. Anything in the garbage can was fair game.

Besides that, Rex had a proclivity for a particular female item that gets thrown into the trash. Sooner or later, if I didn't do something, I'd be embarrassed by what he left in the living room.

I checked around and found a store that said they could custom-make a top for the garbage can. A week later, I picked up the snugly-fitting Plexiglas. I was quite pleased with myself that I had solved this seemingly insurmountable problem. I don't know why I didn't go to the store and get a garbage can with a top. I guess that would have been too easy. My daughters tell me I make my life complicated.

But I did solve the problem—for two years. We had no more garbage can incidents until Rex figured out that if he tipped the garbage can over, the top would fly off, and all the trash would spill out.

So I wised up. This time I went to the store and bought a garbage can that came with a top that clipped on, and that was the end of Rex's garbage siphoning days.

One day Rex did something a little out of character. I never had him fixed, so he had a keen nose for females. That's the only reason I can think of why he went for a solo walk. When I couldn't find him, I grew concerned. Then I discovered the gate was left open. So I walked down the street calling for him, but he didn't come. Getting more worried, I paced the neighborhood for over an hour.

When I'd almost lost hope, thinking someone must have stolen him, I headed home in tears. Then I heard a whimper. That sounded like Rex three houses down the street.

I called his name again and listened. I looked around, but I didn't see him. He whined a third time, and I realized he might be inside my neighbor's closed garage. How did he get stuck in there?

I rushed over and rang my neighbor's doorbell. "I think my dog is in your garage. Can you check?"

Surprised, he went inside to open the garage, and out popped Rex, quite delighted I'd come to rescue him. I was ecstatic and relieved to have my dog back.

"I just closed the garage door," my neighbor said.

I never knew why Rex went into the neighbor's garage unless he was looking for a female. Maybe he missed Shelley so much he decided to go gallivanting for a beauty like she was, but I don't know what he expected to find in the garage.

There was another incident with Rex that was a little embarrassing. My oldest daughter went to public school for kindergarten and first grade. During first grade, they had a "bring-your-pet-to-school day."

So I brought Rex to my daughter's class. Rex was a beautiful Sheltie, well-behaved from his obedience training, and loved kids. I couldn't imagine anything going wrong.

A few days before I took Rex, as part of our summer routine, I had him shaved. It's sweltering hot in Florida during the summer. The first time I had his fur removed, he was so embarrassed when I showed up to take him home, he'd barely looked at me.

Despite his perceived disgrace at being shaved, Rex soon discovered he liked having short hair during the summer. He was more comfortable and more refreshed with all that dense fur gone, and it helped with fleas. Back then, there weren't any flea medicines that worked.

I stayed for the "show and tell" that would take place on the playground, midmorning. Several children had brought their pets, and I wanted to enjoy all the festivities, plus I was one of two room mothers, which meant I should be there to help. The teachers appreciated the extra eyes and hands with the children for social events or seasonal activities.

The big moment came, and the teacher ushered the children outside to view all the pets. I took Rex out of his crate, and he pretended to be Best in Show, strutting around like he was the children's favorite.

All the kids wanted to touch him. My daughter enjoyed showing off her dog, and I was thrilled because Rex loved the children doting on him. He was smiling from ear to ear. Then I saw his "thing." I wanted to hide in my car.

Fortunately, the teachers were somewhere else, and the kids were young, but I never expected that to happen. Bliss enveloped him in historic proportions.

Perhaps I've always been a dog lover at heart because dogs need to be loved. They're dependent creatures, unable to survive in the world on their own. They need people to adopt them, especially from humane societies and pounds, and other nonprofit organizations that do as much as they can on a minimal budget.

But cats are a different story. Cats need to be loved, too, and there are never enough forever families for them either, but they are more independent than dogs and much more resourceful—and maybe even smarter. I would soon learn all about cats.

22
ABBEY

Abby

Shelley had been gone for several months when, on one sunny day, my daughter and I went to the grocery store. As we carted groceries back to the car, we passed a young boy sitting out front with a box of kittens.

When I left home for the grocery store, I had no plans to come home with a kitten, but I couldn't resist taking a peek at the little felines. I became more interested in the fur balls than in my frozen veggies and ice cream.

"Can we get one?" my five-year-old daughter asked.

My mind swirled. I should have bought kitten food when I was in the grocery store.

"Which one is the sweetest one?" I asked the boy, who was about eight. I didn't see his parents, but I sensed they were nearby.

His forlorn face said more than a thousand words. He pointed at a gray, tabby cat, beautifully striped with a distinguished "M" on the forehead.

I reached over and patted the kitten's head. I didn't know the sex. Their anatomy is different from a dog. How did you even tell on a cat?

"Can I pick it up?" I asked.

The little boy nodded.

I held Abbey gently in my hands—I'd already named her, assuming it must be a girl.

"I want to hold her," my daughter said.

As she sat in the grocery cart, she stroked the kitten with a tenderness that melted my heart.

"Can we get her?" my daughter asked excitedly. "Can we get her?"

How could we walk away now? "How much are they?" I asked, noticing the word "free" on a small sign as the words came out of my mouth.

"They are free," he said.

I leaned into the little boy, his eyes locked on Abbey. Grief flooded his face.

"She's your favorite, isn't she?"

The little boy nodded as tears welled up in his eyes.

"I promise I'll take good care of your favorite cat."

He nodded again.

I told him to let me run back into the grocery store to purchase some kitten food. We came out with more than food—kitty toys, and a bowl, and a bed, and catnip.

My daughter bobbed up and down and chattered about her kitten all the way to the car. I remembered her love for cats when I adopted her—her excitement every time she spotted a feline and the catalog she pored over. I had planned on getting a kitten someday, but Shelley had been gone only a short while, and I hadn't thought that far ahead. I knew this was the perfect kitten, and I was thrilled to make my daughter's dreams come true.

After that day, I never saw the little boy again, but I was determined to keep my word. When we introduced the kitten to Rex, he wagged his tail in anticipation of a new playmate. We set up a spot for Abbey in my daughter's bedroom. My five-year-old wouldn't settle for anything less.

Later that afternoon, when the kitten was tired and wanted to sleep, we visited some friends who had two cats. I knew very little about kittens and wanted some words of wisdom.

Driving over, I reflected on Abbey being the young lad's favorite kitten. I could already tell Abbey was sweet and gentle, even tolerant of Rex's love licks. The best part was my daughter had the kitten for which she longed.

It didn't take long for Abbey to cuddle up with my daughter at night, and my princess affectionately lavished her with sweet goodnight kisses.

During the day, she would dress Abbey up in doll clothes and strap hats on her furry head. Then my little cat lover would stroll around the house in dress-up clothes pretending she was Abbey's mother and cradle Abbey in her arms.

Abbey especially loved the Fisher-Price dollhouse and would take catnaps inside it. My daughter would tuck the blankets all around her with only her furry little head poking out.

At Christmas, Abbey would crawl under the Christmas tree and nap. She tried to climb up it a few times, so we had to anchor the tree so she couldn't pull it over. Abbey never had a bad day, never got upset, and never demanded anything. We've since learned some cats are high strung and manipulative—but not Abbey.

Abbey always used the litter box like a good cat. We later learned some cats aren't so good about that either.

One day I noticed that Abbey had put on weight. I should have asked my friends how much food to feed a cat. In hindsight, I should have given her "the talk." Unbeknownst to us, she found a boyfriend when we weren't looking.

We arrived home one day, and when I walked into my daughter's bedroom, I saw something small, slick, and black on my daughter's bed. I rushed over to check it out, fearing a rat or a mouse, and, to my dismay, I discovered a baby kitten. I didn't even know Abbey was pregnant. I was so excited I started squealing. My daughter ran into the room and squealed, too.

The black kitten had just arrived, and Abbey was breathing very hard next to her baby on the bed. There was very little mess, which surprised me, but I wanted to move Abbey to a better spot.

I smiled. She chose to deliver her kittens in her favorite place—on my daughter's bed.

I set about fixing up a birthing box, and my assistant brought me everything I needed. We did it in short order before the next kitten arrived.

Soon Abbey popped out another baby, and another baby, handling the whole process without a meow. I couldn't imagine going through all of that without any help.

I called a good friend on the phone to share my excitement, and as I was on the phone, a roach fell off the light when I flipped the switch. I screamed and disconnected the phone.

My friend thought something terrible happened and called back. I found a shoe and chased the roach across the room. In the meantime, Abbey delivered another kitten.

My daughter now considered herself a seasoned cat-midwife having delivered three kittens. She made sure the babies found the "nibbles," as she called them, so they got all the milk they needed.

The next day, after Abbey had rested, I noticed her leaving her babies for a short time and wandering around the house. I guess she needed a break. Soon I discovered she had secretly moved her kittens to underneath my bed.

For the next few days, I'd put them in my daughter's closet in the birthing box we'd made, and when I wasn't looking, Abbey would move her kittens back underneath my bed.

Soon, however, Abbey gave up and was content to settle into her mothering duties in the closet's secluded spot. By now, Rex was quite interested in the new arrivals, and I wanted to make sure the kittens were safe.

Abbey and the babies stayed in the closet den for a couple of weeks, until the kittens opened their eyes. Then they began to crawl around and explore the room, so we moved them into a large crate. They grew up too fast—although Abbey might disagree. Being a mother is quite exhausting, and she took care of her babies like a saint.

I reflected. Why is it the female has to do all that hard work—going through labor, feeding hungry mouths, licking up all their messes—even the afterbirth—and the father skips out to chase another female. Yep, I know all about men skipping out on their mate.

Abbey never told us who the father was. I bet one of my neighbor's eight cats paid us a visit. The suitor must have been handsome—Abbey's babies were beautiful.

I wondered how my princess would say goodbye to the kittens she helped deliver and feed and socialize. I'd fallen in love with them, too, and hated to see them leave. Of course, I'm more sentimental and couldn't resist keeping one of the kittens. We named her Thomasina.

She was the black kitten that I thought was a mouse. Now we had to find homes for the other three. Someone at church agreed to adopt the twin gray cats. The family had acres and acres of land, so I knew they would always have lizards to chase. Only one cat remained that needed a forever home. What about my friendly neighbor with eight cats? Might they want one more? I threw up a prayer. "Dear God...."

23
THOMASINA

Thomasina

M y spiel was perfect as I headed over to my cat friend's house. I crossed my fingers. The little gray and black kitten should melt their hearts. After listening and petting the kitten, my neighbor said he needed to discuss it with his wife.

A few days later, he returned and said they wanted to give the kitten to their mother-in-law. She had just buried her very old cat. I was ecstatic.

Now we had two cats. Would Thomasina be like her mother—

sweet, easy-going, and gentle? From the beginning, Abbey had been perfect. She'd snuggle up with my daughter at night and purr for hours.

When my daughter had a playmate over, she and her friend now each had a cat to pamper. One would put Abbey in the doll's bed, and the other would dress Thomasina up in doll clothes. While one strapped a hat on Abbey's head, the other pushed Thomasina in the baby carriage.

When the cats tired of the attention, they'd retreat to their private hideaway. Each had their favorite spot in the house. Abbey loved the Fisher Price dollhouse, and Thomasina loved the cat hotel.

At Christmastime, we didn't need presents under the tree. We had two cats that took up all that space. When I did find time to wrap gifts, the cats would "play" among the boxes. They'd tear off the bows, jump on them, and use the boxes to climb the tree. They were always drinking out of the Christmas tree water despite a full water bowl.

Thomasina preferred to drape her tail in the water bowl—perhaps to cool off. When Abbey got hot, she'd crawl into the bathroom sink and nap.

Thomasina turned out to be as loving and sweet as her mother. When she'd had her fill playing dress-up, she'd join me in the sunroom, stretch out on the cat hotel, and keep me company while I worked.

We had learned a lot about cats by this point, enough to know that cats can get pregnant before they are grown up—no wonder there are so many homeless cats—so we had Abbey and Thomasina spayed as soon as possible.

When we brought Thomasina home after being fixed, Abbey didn't like her baby anymore. Did Thomasina smell different? Maybe it was an alpha-beta thing.

When I went to Vietnam to adopt my second daughter, I put a photo of Thomasina in my purse as she was catnapping on the cat hotel. Thomasina was so much like her mother that I never knew cats could be anything other than loving, well-behaved, affectionate, and adorable. We were spoiled.

It also never occurred to me that there were hidden dangers in the backyard. Thomasina was a spry little cat and never got into trouble, but one day I couldn't find her.

She had spent the night outside, and the next morning, she didn't come when I called. I looked everywhere. As I cleaned the pool, I wondered, could she be under the pool deck? I left the pole in the pool and stepped down the stairs to look through the wooden deck lattice. There was Thomasina, lying on her side.

I pulled her out and saw that she was gone. How could that be when she had been fine the day before? My older daughter was at school, and the younger one was taking a nap. I cried. I couldn't believe, just like that, Thomasina was gone—so suddenly and so unexpectedly. I would have more tears to dry when I told my daughters.

Later in the day, I dug a shallow grave near the house in a woodsy area. Darkness was near, and I was exhausted. Someday, I'd fix this area up and make it into a beautiful garden. I wanted to preserve the spot where I had buried her.

Years passed before I was able to make good on my promise. As I write this, the garden is beautiful with plantings of Begonias, Pentas, Coleus, Mums, Caladiums, Vinca, Curcuma gingers, ferns, and more. Memorial plaques of all my pets will eventually fill the garden. It's my quiet place of solitude.

Abbey loved to eat, and that was her undoing. If we had put her on a perpetual diet, she would have been a sad cat. My daughter tried for a while. She would place her on the pool railing and coax her to walk along the top.

I'm not sure how much exercise she got, but it was a good start for a fat cat. I guess we were too complicit, letting her lap up all the food she wanted and bask in the Florida sunshine.

Her extra pounds in her later years contributed to diabetes. Much to our disappointment, it's nearly impossible to control diabetes in a cat. We managed for about four or five months, but her quality of life had significantly declined. The day came when I knew we needed to say goodbye. After a couple of episodes with seizures, it seemed inhumane to prolong her life for our sake.

With my two daughters gathered around me, Abbey lay in my lap in the vet's office. We made her comfortable through our tears, letting her know how much we loved her. She slipped from this world in my arms. At eleven, she breathed her last and journeyed over the rainbow bridge where she can eat all she wants.

I kept my word to the little boy at the grocery store who cried when we took Abbey home. Abbey had a good life, and as my first cat, she set a high standard for all the others that followed.

24
MOLLY PART 1

On a whim, I took my seven-year-old daughter to the exotic animal fair at the state fairgrounds. I don't know what possessed me to do that—not that I give a hoot about exotic animals, but Gainesville is a small community. Without The University of Florida and the Gators, Gainesville would be like any other Florida town full of gray-bearded live oaks, snapping alligators, and crystal clear springs.

I love that about Florida, but I also love the international culture, diversity, and emphasis on the arts that The University brings. Since I was homeschooling, I could call it a field trip because we interacted with snakes, lizards, bats, frogs, and unusual breeds of cats.

What happened at the exotic fair was even more consequential than when I drove to Atlanta from Augusta in one car and came home in another. In plain language, I bought a new car without telling my ex-husband. Maybe that's why he divorced me, but I digress.

As we looked at all the displays of weird animals, we came upon the cutest Jack Russell Terriers. I recognized the breed from the *Wishbone T.V.* series. Their small stature, spunkiness, and brown-and-white markings reminded me of Shelley, and their playful antics rejuvenated my desire for another Shelley. Even their facial expressions were a bitter-sweet imitation of my beloved pet.

Despite walking away from the display a couple of times, I returned, each time wanting to adopt one. Eventually, we walked out the door with a Jack Russell puppy.

We headed to the pet store with Molly, the name I gave her, to pick up a few things. That allowed me time to think about introducing Molly to Rex, Abbey, and Thomasina. Hopefully, Molly would be okay with cats. As I drove home, it felt like deja vu. I didn't think this through at all.

My fears were unfounded. All the introductions went well. Introductions always go well with cats when they make themselves invisible. Abbey and Thomasina were smart, and that's what smart cats do.

Molly and Rex hit it off from the beginning. Of course, Rex never met a female he didn't like. We still had Shelley's old crate, and now we were the proud owners of two dogs and two cats. It was uneventful, except for Molly had one crucial thing backward.

Convinced she was supposed to do her elimination in the house, no matter how many times we walked her, she would pee when we brought her inside. When she was outside, she barked at the moon or anything that moved instead of doing her chores. Even if she were out all day, she would squat as soon as we brought her in. She would even wet the crate. That seemed unnatural. Dogs don't want to soil where they sleep.

It didn't take long for me to realize we'd bought Molly from a puppy mill. Puppy mills are notorious for keeping animals in cages and not letting them take care of their personal needs. As a result, dogs learn to soil themselves. It's not a natural dog behavior.

I loved Molly even more because confining a pet in a crate is a form of animal abuse. I wanted to make her happy. She'd probably never had an opportunity to run around outside or bark at squirrels or chase lizards. Despite her questionable beginnings, she was a typical Jack Russell—territorial, loud, and sweet.

Rex was a great companion, but Rex was housetrained, so we brought him in at night and left Molly outside. That was okay until the neighbors complained about her barking.

Then we brought her in the garage and crated her, covering the base with doggie pads. What would we have done without that invention?

Rex was eleven when we adopted Molly, so he was a senior dog, but he lived to the ripe old age of sixteen when he died of old age. Molly and Rex enjoyed the big backyard together for five years. When Rex passed away, Molly still had a large area to romp in, but she was lonely. My Jack Russell no longer had a buddy, and we couldn't bring her in the house. We couldn't even keep her in a crate inside because she would immediately soil it.

We had a friend whose neighbor had a Jack Russell. I called them one day and left a message asking if they would like a second Jack Russell. They called me back and said they'd love to meet Molly, but I couldn't bring myself to part with Molly when that day arrived.

Conflicted, I debated what to do. I loved Molly too much to rehome her, but my heart broke that Molly spent so much time alone. Dogs are social animals, pack animals, whether it's with animal-kind or people. I had two daughters, worked full time, and homeschooled my older one. I felt sad that I couldn't give Molly more attention, but no matter how hard I tried, I couldn't housetrain or crate-train her.

Then I had an idea. Perhaps she might like to be adopted by a horse farm that had several Jack Russells. Molly would have acres to explore, and I believed that would be more pleasurable than living a solitary life in our backyard. The horse farm owners bred Jack Russells, and when they saw photos of her, they wanted her.

We took Molly with us for my daughter's next horseback lesson. We let Molly explore and run around the horse farm during the riding lesson, and when my daughter finished, the horse farm owner held Molly so she couldn't get in the car with us.

I'll never forget the look on Molly's face—why are you leaving me? I told myself she would be happier. She'd have acres to explore and lots of Jack Russells to form a Molly clan, kids to interact with when they came for horseback lessons, and at least a dozen horses to pester.

The owner was someone we'd known for over a year, and while Molly might be sad now, she'd be happy later. And we'd see her when we came for the weekly horseback lesson. I called a couple of times to check on her, and everything seemed to be going well.

I couldn't wait to see Molly again; I missed her more than I anticipated. We still loved her, and I hated her not being with us.

Every week when we arrived at the farm, Molly would greet us as she recognized my car's sound. She loved seeing us and would look forlorn when we left. That part never got easier.

It didn't take long before Molly mothered a litter of gorgeous puppies. I wanted to keep one, but we didn't. Suppose I couldn't housetrain the puppy? I took some photos of Molly with her beautiful progeny before they were adopted. I hoped they went to good homes. Still, I had this unsettled feeling that all was not well with Molly.

25

MOLLY PART 2

A few months passed, and then we discovered Molly was pregnant again, I wasn't happy about the second litter. I never meant for Molly to be used just for breeding. Knowing she came from a puppy mill made me feel like I was perpetuating the problem.

After Molly had her first litter of puppies and her babies were gone, she seemed depressed. She was very proud of her offspring and basked in the limelight when we visited her and her babies in a stable stall. Molly took her mothering duties seriously, proudly showing off her puppies.

On later visits, her eyes were missing that glimmer, as if when her babies were taken away, her joy was gone. She greeted us less and less when we arrived for my daughter's horseback lesson, sometimes only appearing just before we left.

One day when we went to the farm, Molly didn't show up at all. I asked the workers if they knew where she was. I was concerned because she always eventually came around to see us.

I felt overwhelming regret that we had given her to the horse farm, but I didn't feel right asking to have her back. Besides, we'd be in the same situation all over again. She would be alone in the backyard for most of the day and crated at night when we brought her in.

However, I'd seen that look in her eyes too many times, "Why can't I go home with you?" I was sick at heart.

I worried about Molly until we returned the following week. Then we learned why she never greeted us. Someone mistakenly locked Molly up in a storage shed for three days. She almost died and lost that litter of puppies. After that, I had many regrets.

A couple of weeks later, I received a phone call from the farm. "Molly got hit by a car and is at the vet. She is going to lose an eye. We can't keep her away from the highway. We think she's trying to find her way home. Do you want her back?"

We immediately went to the vet. She had already had surgery, and the doctor had bandaged half her face. But she perked up when she saw us, flapping her tail with that glimmer in her good eye once again. I promised her as soon as she was well, we would take her home.

That day came, and I recognized the old Molly I once knew—ecstatic to be going home with the family she loved. Even though she lost the vision in her left eye, she adapted well. Until she was well along in years, her left eye looked completely normal.

We still weren't able to bring her inside—even the horse farm owner lamented that she couldn't housetrain Molly even though all the other Jack Russells were housebroken—but Molly was content to be an outside dog. Within a few months, her year at the horse farm became a distant memory. It was like she had never left.

The owner of the farm later told me the other Jack Russells didn't accept Molly. I guess there is a pecking order in the dog world, and Molly, being an outsider, was at the bottom of the Jack Russell hierarchy.

One day a friend of mine called and said they were going out to some Podunk town to watch Jack Russells compete in agility trials. "You should bring Molly," my friend said. "She would love it."

It didn't take much coaxing to get me to go. Soon we were headed off to an obscure farm in the boonies to show off my Jack Russell's agility talents. I think Molly had more fun that day than at any time in her life. She jumped through all the hoops, competed in several races chasing a fake bunny, and performed spectacular feats I never knew existed.

Even with one eye, she beat some of the other dogs. We drove home at the end of the day exhausted but elated. Molly had proven she was a top agility dog.

Soon we discovered how much Molly loved to play ball. I'd bought a unique ball, and one day when we were in the pool playing with it, it flew out of the water. Molly leaped in the air, punched the ball with her nose, and it plopped back into the pool with a big splash.

After that, we included her in the pool games, throwing the ball to her so she could punch it back. She rarely missed—and "punch ball" with Molly became a family affair. We had to take turns because we all wanted to play with her.

We'd applaud every time the ball landed in the pool. Somewhere we have it on video. I should upload it on YouTube and advertise it, "One Eye Jack Russell Performs Ball Tricks by the Pool."

Would my attitude have been as good as hers if I had only one good eye? When I had shingles, I could have lost vision in my right eye and been like Molly.

I have an author friend who lost her eyesight in her forties due to a congenital condition. At first, I didn't know she was blind. I met her at a writer's conference when she spoke to a roomful of wannabe bestsellers. She didn't allow herself to be a victim of her blindness. She rose above it.

The two middle school girls who used to walk Rex for me were now teens, and they continued to come over and walk Molly. I'd hear the knock on the door in the afternoons. "Can we take Molly for a walk?"

I remembered how I used to walk Gypsy. Back then, I thought walking dogs was a kid thing. Now, however, it's America's new pastime. Instead of raising kids, people adopt dogs and raise them as surrogate children. Recently I saw a "dog nursery school." If I were a dog, I'd gone in there to sniff it out.

In all those years, Molly only had one other issue until she developed bone cancer at sixteen—a decade after we brought her home from the horse farm. She had a problem with "stuckness."

One day, I noticed Molly was squatting as female dogs do, but she left no evidence behind. I soon realized she had a bigger problem than I could solve.

Off to the vet we went to have her checked. Molly was quite indignant about having that part of her body examined, and soon they took her into a private room for a more invasive procedure. I didn't want to think about what that might be. I just wanted her to be able to poop again. Strange how unimportant things become very important when something goes wrong.

After a few worried minutes waiting, the tech and Molly returned. Molly was all smiles wagging her tail. I took that as a hopeful sign that she felt better.

When the doctor appeared, she related Molly's delicate situation. "I had to reach up there and pull it out," the vet said, or words to that effect. "It was really stuck up there."

Soon we were giving Molly "unstuck" medicine so she wouldn't have that "stuck" problem to crop up again. The prescription cost me a pretty penny.

When Molly was sixteen, she developed a limp. At first, we treated her with anti-inflammatories, but we went back to the vet when that didn't help. This time the vet took X-rays. I sat in the waiting room for the results. The tech returned with Molly, and she wagged her tail, once again, with that hopeful look that things would be okay, like when she had the "stuck" problem.

The vet reappeared shortly with X-rays in hand and slid them on the lightbox. She pointed out the problem and informed me of the dire prognosis. I couldn't believe what I was hearing.

How could a simple limp turn into bone cancer? I suppose it showed on my face because Molly's happy countenance disappeared, too, and she quit wagging her tail.

She knew I couldn't fix her this time and make her limp go away. The worst feeling in the world is when you can't fix something because it's unfixable.

However, that day of sad news was still lightyears away. Until then, God never meant for Molly to live out her days alone in the backyard. She needed a friend, and we found the perfect one for her at the Humane Society.

26
BOOTS AND TINKERBELL

Boots

My cat-loving daughter was in a very talkative mood one day when I brought her home from gymnastics. "My coach says a friend of hers has two kittens that need a home."

"Where did she get them?" I asked.

"The mother cat got run over, and the kittens were beside their dead mother. My coach's friend rescued them and brought them home. But her mother won't let her keep them. If she can't find them homes, she'll have to take the kittens to the pound."

I hate to admit it, but I'm as predictable as needing my dark chocolate Klondike ice cream bar once a day. Well, I guess there are worse things to be addicted to, but four words in the same sentence—dog, cat, homeless, and pound—afflict my heart every time.

"I'm sure they'll find them a home," I reassured her. I thought the mother would cave in and let her daughter keep them. What mother could be so cruel as to take helpless kittens to the pound?

I didn't hear anything more for a few days, and then my daughter reminded me of the homeless kittens. "They haven't found homes for them, and tomorrow, she's taking them to the pound."

I pictured in my mind two sweet kittens suffering a terrible fate—death. This was back when Alachua County euthanized over half of the homeless animals. How could I not help?

"If they can't find homes for them," I told her, "then we'll take them and find homes."

Soon I had two kittens, a male and a female. They were bigger than I imagined they'd be, past that cute stage and more like grown-up cats, which meant they would be harder to place. I went to my cat neighbors again, who had bailed me out twice before. This time I wasn't as lucky.

I asked the church administrator, a huge cat lover, "Do you want a sweet, lovable black kitten? You can even have your choice of a male or female."

The male cat had a little bit of white fur on his paws, so we named him Boots. We called the female Tinkerbell after a dog my mom had when I was a baby.

Tinkerbell

The cat lover church administrator smiled broadly. I knew that meant no. How could she say no so nicely? I've yet to figure out how to do that. I guess that's why she's the church administrator, and I'm not. I asked all my friends but had no takers.

Then I asked another neighbor I hadn't badgered before if she would take one, and I would keep the other one. She said yes. She wanted the male, which was fine, and we adopted Tinkerbell, the female.

Tinkerbell adjusted well to Abbey and the dogs, and I assumed

Boots was doing great over at my neighbor's. No news is good news, I thought.

A few days later, I was working in the sunroom, and I saw a black cat looking inside the window at me. What was Boots doing over here?

I carried him back over to my neighbor's, but every day he returned. I'd see him looking at me through the window as he precariously balanced himself on the fence railing.

I guess he had decided he didn't want to live at my neighbor's. He wanted to live with us. A couple of weeks passed as I forged a foot trail to my neighbor's house until we knew it was useless to take him over there.

I've seen it too many times. If cats don't like where they're living, they'll find another place to their liking. It's no big deal to them. Boots loved living with us.

Tinkerbell loved her home here until a day came when she seemed to say, "You've got too many cats around here. I'm headed off to catless pastures."

I admit we did end up with too many cats for a time. It reminds me of that old nursery rhyme about the old woman in the shoe.

> There was an old woman who lived in a shoe.
> She had so many children she didn't know what to do.
> She gave them some broth without any bread;
> Then whipped them all soundly and put them to bed.

I'm glad I didn't know those last two lines when I was young. They're dreadful. The first two lines, though, upset me even as a child. How could a mother not know how to take care of her children? It seemed heartless, and I would ponder as a child those poor children with an incompetent mother.

Well, I was determined not to be an old cat woman with so many cats she didn't know what to do. I told myself, after we got Boots and Tinkerbell, no more cats.

I informed my daughters, "This is it. No more cats. No more dogs. I'm not going to be like that old woman in the shoe."

"Who is that?" my daughter asked. I'd made sure I never read them that nursery rhyme.

With some experience behind me with cats, I knew about getting our little critters fixed, so I had Tinkerbell spayed and Boots neutered. Of course, Boots was my first male cat, and as I soon learned, male cats are a wee bit different from female cats.

My cat daughter went with me to pick up Boots from the vet to hold him on the way home. Everything seemed fine when we left the vet but quickly deteriorated. I guess he had a full bladder because I looked over at my daughter and saw a fountain of water gushing forth. "Don't let it get on the car seat," I told her. "Just let him pee on you."

It would be easier to wash it off her than to remove the stench from the seat cushion. Those clothes never got worn again, but my car didn't know anything different. He had perfect aim.

A couple of years later, my cat daughter approached me about getting a female kitten—a teeny, tiny kitten from the Humane Society for a birthday present. Of course, I said no.

She persisted, insisting that was all she wanted. What was I thinking when I changed my mind and said yes?

27

LILY AND SIRIUS

M y cat-loving, resourceful daughter—and both could claim to be that daughter, so I'm not giving away any secrets—sweet-talked me into getting a kitten. She remembered the days long ago when she was a top-notch kitten nanny and hoped to experience the joys of cat motherhood once more.

We hopped into my green 2001 Sienna—that I've driven around the world ten times—and we took a short trip to the Humane Society. If a kitten needed a home, God would have the purr-fect kitten for my daughter.

Now, I know I can't go to the Humane Society unless I plan to adopt an animal, and I can't foster either, but we were getting a kitten on this trip. So I wasn't doing anything on a whim. I planned this all out for my daughter's birthday.

We arrived, and my daughter went inside the cat motel, and I went to check out the dog dormitory—I was just curious. The first holding cell I came to exhibited an adorable black and white dog that reminded me of Shelley. He was Shelley's size, and even his sweet face resembled my dog of nineteen years. He looked at me with brown, hopeful eyes, wagged his bushy tail, and traipsed back and forth, revealing a spunky personality. He was so enthusiastic to see me. I wanted to hold him.

Even though he was the same size as Shelley, I didn't realize he would grow into a big dog—and he didn't tell me. I guess he knew that if he imitated Shellie in size, personality, and looks, he'd have an outstanding chance of winning my heart.

I asked the volunteer if I could hold him. She brought him out of the pen, and I sat in a chair as she placed him in my lap. He thumped his tail across my thighs and licked my cheeks. If he had been applying for a job, I would have checked off all the boxes, "top candidate." He charmed me to the hilt, wiggling in my lap as one happy fellow, and I was smitten with his outgoing personality.

Of course, I'd adopted Molly from an exotic animal show because she reminded me of Shelley. What are the odds I'd stumble upon two dogs that harkened back to my companion for so many years? Either of them could've been a Bulldog or a Pitbull or less spirited, or meek and mild. Those are delightful dogs, I'm sure, but better suited for others.

I sweet-talked him as I sat in the chair, asking him where he came from and what his favorite food was—okay, maybe I didn't ask him about his favorite food, but how could such a gorgeous, friendly dog like him end up at the Humane Society? Perhaps that should have been my first hint of surprises.

As I basked in his flirtatious bid for a home, I'd forgotten about my daughter in the cat motel. This little dog had captured my heart. I toyed with the idea of adopting him. Except—I was already adopting a cat. Did I want to go home with a dog and a cat?

I considered all the extra vet bills and food costs, and that little voice of wisdom accused me of insanity. Then I thought about Molly. She needed a playmate. Soon my daughter reappeared as I sat in the chair holding the black and white, homeless, winsome canine.

She gave me one of those looks. "You aren't getting that dog, are you?"

"Maybe." I was still considering it. He would make the third dog I'd adopted without the slightest inkling ahead of time. I seemed to have an uncanny history of doing that.

All of them had worked out, though, even with Molly's un-housetraining. Now that I was holding this little fellow, how could I let someone else adopt him? Suppose they mistreated him? I would always wonder.

Besides that, I'd gone halfway around the world to adopt two daughters. This wasn't as big a deal.

"Did you find the kitten you want?"

"Yes," she said. "I want you to see her."

I gave the homeless dog back to the tech and told her I'd return in a moment. My daughter took me into the kitten room, and sure enough, there was this beautiful, mostly white feline with a little black fur on her head, two other large black spots, and a couple of smaller brown spots.

She was delicately feminine and had the softest fur of any cat I'd ever touched. Of course, how do you not fall in love with such an eye-catching kitten? You don't see many like that. Most cats are black or gray.

"That's the one you want?"

My daughter nodded.

The little kitten was a beauty, and to see the excitement on my daughter's face was confirmation enough. The volunteer started preparing the paperwork, and I went back to the dog dormitory. The black and white cuddly canine was back on the concrete floor, all by himself, looking sad. When he saw me in the doorway, he jumped up, wagged his tail, and locked his eager eyes on mine. "Can I go home with you?"

The volunteer stood beside me. "Have you made a decision?"

I nodded. "Yep, we're adopting the kitten and the dog."

Soon I was filling out his paperwork, too, and my mind raced faster than the speed of light. When we arrived home, I realized I needed another crate as we only had one that we used for Molly. We went to the store, and I bought a small crate for him. I thought he was full grown. Three weeks later, he'd outgrown it.

And he kept growing. "How big is he going to get?" I asked the vet.

"Oh, he looks like a Border Collie mix, maybe some Australian Shepherd."

"How big do they get?" I knew Collies were large dogs. I tried to imagine my cute little puppy that looked like Shelley when I brought him home growing into a big dog. I'd never had a large dog, except when I was a teen. We had Gretchen, the German Shepherd, and Tasha, the Samoyed; and, after that, the whole house was full of champion Samoyeds.

I never did get an exact answer, only that he had big paws. Big paws meant he would grow into his paws. He kept evolving, and soon he became as big as a Collie.

My daughter had officially taken over the naming duties, and being a huge Harry Potter fan, she named him Sirius. I still struggle with spelling that name, but that was his name. Everyone wanted to spell it like the word "serious," but he was not a serious dog. I'm not a Harry Potter fan—I fell asleep during one of the movies, but my daughter read every book start to finish.

I've wondered what kind of character Sirius was in the books. I can vouch that our Sirius was one of a kind. He was smart, charming, and loyal. Those were his good qualities.

On the flip side, however, I never knew a dog that could be so obstinate. Sirius was witty and cunning, and he knew it. He was as secretive as a thief and as stubborn as a mule. Put all of that together, and that makes for one swell dog.

Where do I begin with Sirius? Sirius needed to be outside. He had more energy bottled up in that athletic body than a rocket blasting off from the earth.

He had a voracious appetite for items deemed inedible—phone cords, satellite wires, cable connectors, shoes, socks, sandals, books, toys, patio doors, porch screens, CD covers, plastic containers, crayons, hats, sticks, shoes, pencils, books, and anything else he could wrap his mouth around.

He destroyed the porch door, the screen siding on the porch, the grill cover multiple times—I can't remember how many times I replaced it—and his favorite place to pee in the yard was on the air conditioner—the perfect height on which to raise his leg. The air conditioner man told me I needed to keep my dog from peeing on it. I sighed. How do you teach a dog something like that?

He dug holes to get out of the yard. He knew how to open closed doors. He could scamper under the garage door cracked only high enough for a cat. I'd have friends over, and he'd eat their shoes if they took them off while we enjoyed dinner. He'd steal game parts while we were playing and tear them to shreds. Once I had to replace somebody's game when he ate a vital card.

As a broadcast captioner, those telephone and satellite wires were pretty important—if I wanted to buy his dogfood. I got to know the phone and satellite maintenance specialists on a first-name basis. What would I have done without my next-door handyman who fixed everything Sirius ate or destroyed?

I learned never to leave the chicken out on the kitchen counter. That was Sirius' favorite dish. One day I brought home a roasted chicken from the Fresh Market. I set it on the table, and then remembered I forgot something. I returned to the grocery store, and when I came home, the chicken was no longer on the countertop where I thought I'd left it.

Perplexed, I turned and saw the remnants of the cardboard container strewn across the dining room floor into my bedroom. I followed the evidence and found the thief gulping down the chicken, bones and all. My roasted chicken dinner was in Sirius's happy belly.

I went back to the Fresh Market to get another chicken, and guess what? All the roasted chickens were gone. There wasn't a single one left. When I returned home, I scolded him, "Shame on you, Sirius," but he just gave me that apologetic look as he licked his chops.

He ducked his head in fake remorse as if to say, "I'm sorry." He knew he'd been a bad boy, but he also knew how big my heart was. We ate half a dinner that night—pure vegetarian.

Several months later, he did the same thing again. You'd think I would've learned not to leave my roasted chicken dinner on the countertop. Again, I'd forgotten something and went back to the store. And again, I returned to find my dinner in his belly.

Instead of telling him, "Shame on you, Sirius," I told myself, "Shame on me."

After that, when I bought a roasted chicken, I'd stick it in the microwave until we were ready to eat. And I'd tell my would-be dog thief, "No, you aren't eating roasted chicken for dinner tonight. That's my dinner."

He'd walk away disappointed. He hated it when I outsmarted him.

28
SIRIUS' SHENANIGANS

Sirius was Molly's best friend, and they hung out in their favorite places in the back and side yard during the hot, lazy summers and nippy, mild winters. That was back when I had no weeds and no grass because they were my weed stompers and hole diggers. So I let the naturalness of native habitat create an oasis of green fauna.

Despite Sirius's palatial environs, it wasn't enough to curb his sense of entitlement. He took great delight in challenging my authority. Or perhaps as a herding dog, he wanted to herd me into his idea of compliance.

When my daughter was about five, we returned home from running errands one day, and she belted out orders like I was her minion. I loosened my seatbelt and sat there for a minute until she finished. Then I turned around and said, "There is only one person in charge here, and it's not you."

I told Sirius that, too, but he was too obstinate to listen. I needed help, so we took Sirius to obedience training at PetSmart.

Humbled, I sat in a chair in a circle with a dozen other dogs with their chastened owners. After a year of dog show classes in my youth and winning ribbons at dog obedience trials with Rex, I needed to go back to the basics. All that stuff I knew about training didn't work with my stubborn Border Collie.

Sirius was interested in the dog bones, dog toys, and dog treats that were strategically placed along the aisles so a dog could sniff out the enticing odors. Sirius took what he wanted. More than once, I'd be at the check-out counter, and the cashier would ask me if I was getting what my dog had in his mouth.

"What do you mean?" I'd ask, and I'd look down at him. He'd pulled something off the rack.

He wanted to introduce himself to every dog in the obedience class and smell them, and everything that moved caught his attention. When it came to the obedience part, he wasn't interested in any of that. He had no intention of following the rules. If they had given out ribbons for placement, Sirius would have come in last.

The dog instructor suggested Sirius might do better with whistle training. She gave me the name of a trainer who'd come out to my house and show me what to do without all the store's distractions.

A week later, the instructor arrived. I soon discovered he was an excellent whistleblower. He taught me how to blow a whistle and click a clicker, but I'm not sure Sirius really "got" it.

After three days, all that training left my head, and I was a hundred dollars poorer. I threw the whistle in the kitchen drawer and gave up. I'd just love him so much he would want to obey me, right? Maybe that would work.

I decided he had far too much energy for our big backyard, so I joined a dog park for $30 per month. The first day I took him, he ran and ran. I could see all that destructive behavior turning into constructive energy. I should have brought him here sooner.

When I was ready to leave, however, he wouldn't come. So my joy in seeing him run around the park had turned into irritation. I hadn't planned on spending thirty minutes chasing him.

Once, he got tangled up in a briar patch and briars covered him from head to tail. I had to painstakingly remove them from his coat. Another time, he went swimming in the mud hole.

I learned early on I had to bathe him before I could put him in my car. I bought tickets for the bath and grooming salon, and he loved that. After a while, he learned he had a nice bath awaiting him, and he was more willing to leave when I called, but I still had to allow at least an hour to catch him and bathe him.

Of course, taking Sirius anywhere was an ordeal. He always got carsick, and I'd have a mess to clean up. I started putting him in a crate to transport him, but I had a hard time getting the container in and out. Where is a guy when you need one?

Eventually, I learned that he would travel in the van best if I put him in the very back. It seemed like the worst place, but he never got carsick back there. He'd just drool all over the place. When I'd put the air conditioner on full blast, that helped.

I took Molly with us a couple of times, but I had a hard time taking both dogs. One of my daughters needed to help me, and neither wanted to spend their Saturday afternoons walking around a poopy dog park with a poopy bag in hand.

This was back in the day before iPhones, and I needed something to do while there. Someone once told me that when you raise kids, everybody does about the same thing, but when your kids leave home, you start being more than a mother or a father and return to some of those hobbies or activities you did before having kids.

I wrote a lot as a kid, and as I followed Sirius around the park, making sure he stayed out of trouble, I'd listen to recordings of authors on cassette tapes. That's how long I've been trying to learn how to write. Someday if I become famous, my word of advice will be: walk around a dog park with a cassette player in one hand and a poopy bag in the other.

Shortly after I started going to the dog park, another woman showed up with her Border Collie. Her dog was young, like Sirius. So we'd sit and talk about how crazy our dogs were. I was relieved to know I wasn't the only one with a Border Collie driving me insane.

The best thing about Sirius was he loved me, and he loved Molly. They were inseparable, and he was Molly's best friend. The two of them kept each other company outside and dug holes and hid bones and chewed on anything they could find.

I am still finding things all these years later, hidden underneath the sandy dirt that they buried. And, in retrospect, after going a year and a half without a dog, I appreciate even more the ruckus dogs make. They instinctively bark at unfamiliar noises, and that's reassuring, knowing that wanna-be thieves would probably go to easier-to-rob pastures.

One day, I decided to test Sirius and see just how much of a watchdog he was. A Star Wars stand-up poster arrived from somewhere, and my daughter, a Star Wars geek, left it out on display in the living room.

The poster stand-up was of a Star Wars lightsaber-wielding character that probably everybody would recognize but me. The image was about seven feet tall. I moved the poster up a few feet from the garage doorway, and when Sirius walked inside, I hid behind the cardboard and shook it, shouting something stupid.

My poor Border Collie shook all over. Sirius wasn't an attack dog after all—he was a wimp. I slid out from behind the poster and reassured him I was the would-be thief.

As I comforted him, I stepped in something wet. My goodness. He was so scared he'd peed on the floor.

After a hug and a kiss, he forgave his idiotic owner. I cleaned up the mess, and we were friends again. Maybe once, though, I got even with him.

Sirius did not like alarms, particularly fire alarms, and we had the most sensitive fire alarm in the universe. You could fry an egg, and the fire alarm would go off. Talk about loud—the entire neighborhood could hear it. Even when you stopped cooking, it would sound for another ten or fifteen minutes.

Soon I was reluctant to use the oven. I sure couldn't cook those frozen apple turnovers I loved. Every time I tried, it would set off the alarm. When I didn't feel like cooking, that was my excuse, that I'd set off the fire alarm, but my daughters loved to cook.

Many times, I'd be on the air captioning, and the fire alarm would go off. Sirius, who often took naps beside me while I worked, would freak out, and the talking heads on T.V. wouldn't stop long enough so I could put him out of my bedroom that doubled as my office.

One day the alarm sounded, and we weren't even cooking. I searched the house for the culprit and discovered a candle burning over the fireplace in the living room.

Sirius was nowhere to be found. I checked the bathtub—one of his favorite places to hide until the danger passed. He wasn't there. I knew he wasn't under my desk. Sometimes, if I wasn't on the air, he'd sneak underneath there and hide. Inevitably, he'd disconnect something, and then the next time I captioned, something important would be unplugged. I'd have to crawl underneath my desk to figure it out.

This time I found him in the kitchen. Not only was he shaking, but his teeth were chattering. I didn't know teeth could do that. I felt sorry for him, but we couldn't turn off the alarm. I coaxed Sirius outside, and several minutes later, he calmed down, much to my relief.

Not long after that, the alarm went off again for no reason, and it wouldn't stop. I listened to it all day—and so did my neighbors. I called my fix-it man, and he came by with a brand-new fire alarm. I never knew life could be so much less stressful with a fire alarm that wasn't activated by a smidgen of smoke, and Sirius was quite appreciative that doomsday quit arriving.

At night I'd bring Molly and Sirius in the garage. I always thought before we showed dogs that putting a dog in a crate was inhumane, but Molly and Sirius loved their "little hideouts."

Sirius had a beautiful bed, and Molly slept on a pee pad. We could have brought Sirius inside as he housetrained himself, but he and Molly were so close, they didn't want to be separated.

Sirius always wanted to make sure Molly was okay. He herded her like she was cattle, as well as our cats. I lamented I didn't have a job for him to do. If only we lived on a farm....

Molly thought Sirius was the most fabulous dog on earth, and she wanted to do whatever Sirius did. However, sometimes what Sirius did wasn't a bright idea. He could be a terrible influence on Molly. Did I say terrible?

29
SIRIUS' ESCAPADES

Besides being hard-headed, stubborn, and deaf when he wanted to be, Sirius was fiercely loyal. He was also quite amusing. I bought him many bones and toys to chew on through the years. Those he didn't consume, he would bury. He especially loved the soup bones from my Christmas homemade vegetable soup. I made it only once a year.

I would buy five or six beef bone packages from Publix and boil them in water until all the marrow was separated from the bones. Then I'd remove the bones from the homemade broth and let them cool. Once I knew they wouldn't burn his mouth, I'd give him two or three freshly cooked bones, and Molly also got her share of beef bones. They'd go find some corner off to themselves and chew on them for hours.

After distributing passels of bones for a couple of days, I'd freeze the rest. Throughout the year, I'd unthaw them and reward Molly and Sirius. That was their favorite treat, and because the bones never got consumed, they would bury them in the yard.

One time I brought home a rubber chicken I'd bought at PetSmart. The rubber chicken was quite large and made funny, screeching noises.

Molly and Sirius must have thought it was real. How would they know the difference since they'd never had a live chicken?

There was only one problem—I had two dogs and one chicken, a serious matter for who gets the prize. They'd never had a chicken to fight over. One of them had the head; the other had the toes. And they pulled and pulled and pulled that thing as it screeched to the high heavens.

Suddenly and quite unexpectedly, the chicken exploded. Sirius had one half, and Molly had the other. They both won that battle.

Another day when I was at PetSmart, I saw a tasty-looking bone. Even to me, it looked delicious. I bought it and offered it to Sirius when I got home, and he snatched it and took off for a chewy evening. After a while, he decided he wanted to save the rest, but he couldn't figure out where to hide it. I think he was afraid the cats would steal his bone.

I confess. Sometimes Sirius' mastication imprints were very odious, and I'd throw the half-chewed bones away and give him a new one. He especially liked those pig ears; they were the worst. I don't think he ever figured out I was disposing his bones. He thought the cats were stealing them.

He picked up his bone and traipsed from one room to another. I watched as he hid it behind the dining room chair—nope, that wasn't any good. I could see it in his eyes—the cats would find it.

He retrieved it and paced back and forth in the living room before disappearing in the back. I figured he must be checking out the bathroom. That was his favorite place to hide during a thunderstorm, so he knew that room well. My daughters usually kept their bedroom doors shut, so that wasn't an option.

Then I heard him putting his bone in his empty food bowl. I thought that would satisfy him, but no, the cats might want to eat his food—although they had plenty of their own.

He must have spent ten or fifteen minutes trying to find the perfect place to hide his bone for a rainy day. In the meantime, my daughter pulled out her iPhone and started videotaping him.

I could hear him getting more desperate, whimpering, and pacing back and forth from the living room to the dining room to the kitchen to the sunroom where I was.

I knew he'd found the perfect spot when he stopped whimpering. The house became quiet. Too quiet.

Where did he put it? I got up and walked into the living room. He stood there with a happy, satisfied look. No bone protruded from his mouth, so I knew he'd done something with it. I glanced around but saw no bone.

I checked behind the sofa, his food dish, and underneath the entertainment center. I moved the couch away from the wall., and all I saw was dog fur.

"Sirius, where's your bone?"

He looked up at me with those big brown eyes, tail wagging.

Then I lifted the sofa cushion. Suddenly my panicked dog jumped on the sofa, and all I could see was his rump in the air and a face buried beneath the sofa cushion. Sirius popped back out, and his desperate, wild eyes flashed around the room. Bone-in-mouth, he barged off to find another place to hide it.

I felt terrible for discovering his hidden bone. That was the perfect spot, and I'd spoiled it. A couple of minutes later, he came trotting back into the living room carrying his bone. He seemed to be in a much better frame of mine, and he jumped back on the sofa. Soon his bone was back in the same spot, underneath the pillow. I promised him I wouldn't tell the cats where he hid it.

As much as Sirius loved bones, there was something else he enjoyed more—launching a great escape and making me chase him, and there was nothing that frustrated me more.

Of course, there was the one time he went nowhere except the front yard. He laid down a few yards from the street but refused to come inside when I called him. While I was trying to get him in, a police car drove by.

We have leash laws in Alachua County, and when the police officer saw my dog off a leash in my front yard, he stopped out front and parked. Now I knew I had to get Sirius inside, but he refused to come. If he left the yard, the police officer could file a report. Or haul him off in his car, or call the pound, or something—Lord knows what. I called and called for my thick-headed Border Collie to come. He wouldn't budge.

What was that police officer doing in front of my house, anyway? He must be bored. Why didn't he chase some thief or robber? Was the county that desperate for work they had to park in front of my house and arrest my dog?

After fifteen minutes, the police officer drove away. In the darkness, Sirius was still lounging as the stars peeked out. I took a shower, partly to let off steam—nothing like a pleasant shower to cool you down—and when I came back into the living room, I saw Sirius through the window still relaxing on the St. Augustine grass. I opened the front door and called once more, "Sirius."

He immediately tore through the front yard and came inside. After a good scolding, I put him to bed. Deep down, I was glad he was safe. He never did anything like that again. When he got out after that, typically, he took off for the hinterlands.

One day I was captioning, but I was only doing cut-ins and had about twenty-five minutes till my next cut-in. I needed to pick up my daughter from gymnastics. I had plenty of time because she was only two streets over. I pulled out of our subdivision and headed south on Southwest 51st Street. As I was driving, I saw a dog that looked remarkably like Sirius trotting down the sidewalk. I wondered how a dog could look so similar to mine and live so close.

Wait a minute. I did a double take. That was Sirius! I pulled into the side street and jumped out of my car. "Sirius," I called as I ran toward him.

My Border Collie ran away. What was I going to do? I didn't have time to chase him. My angst kicked into high gear. How did he get out of the yard? I tried to catch him but to no avail.

I was already cooking in the hot Florida sunshine, partly from the heat and partly from anger. My stubborn, strong-willed dog was going to get me into trouble with my job. I didn't have time for this.

As I chased him, I saw a young man walking toward Sirius. He sized up the situation pretty quickly. I'm sure my red-hot face and footsteps made it evident I had a runaway dog, and I was desperate.

Of course, I had no leash, so I don't know what I thought I'd use to retrieve him with, but he was wearing a collar.

The man took off after Sirius and tackled him straight on like a football player. He clasped Sirius by the collar and held him until I got there.

"Let me get my van and move it closer." I ran to my car, and the man helped me to get Sirius inside. What would I have done had he not come along right then?

Sirius was seriously a con artist. He learned how to tell when a door wasn't tightly closed, how to scoot underneath the garage door when I cracked it for the cats, how to bang on the fence gate until it broke—that happened a few times—and if someone was hauling the trash out and didn't close the front door, or the wind blew the door open, he'd run out.

Rex, my Shetland Sheepdog, had escaped only once, and that was when he got shut up in my neighbor's garage. He never went anywhere again. Shelley never got out. But then—there was Gypsy, the other con artist in my life.

I guess God knew I could handle it; He had more confidence in me than I had in myself.

30
THE GREAT ADVENTURE

One bright, sunny day, Sirius exceeded his badness by a multiplier of ten. He went on his greatest escapade, but this time, it wasn't just him. He enticed Molly to go with him.

Molly would never leave the yard, especially with only one eye—at least not after the horse farm debacle. She had no desire to go anywhere—except to be with Sirius. Her favorite place in the world was in the backyard.

To my astonishment, I fortuitously caught Sirius and Molly running up the street toward the subdivision entrance. Sirius was on a dog mission as he galloped up the road. Molly was doing her best to follow him. With her shorter legs, she couldn't run as fast, but she could still outrun me.

What was I going to do? I had two dogs to chase down. I grabbed the leashes and took off after them, but soon they were going in different directions. Where were my daughters when I needed them?

In an instant, my dogs disappeared, and I was frantic. I roamed up and down the neighborhood streets calling out their names. I asked the neighbors if they had seen two dogs. Blank looks told me they hadn't. Then I got in my car and started driving the roads, calling one name and then the other. I drove for over an hour without any luck. I was upset at Sirius for coaxing Molly to go with him. Besides that, Molly had already proven herself to be dumb about cars. I feared her getting hit again. Now I was looking for dead dogs in the road as much as live dogs.

I drove down unfamiliar streets and hollered to folks working in their yard, "Have you seen two dogs, a Jack Russell and a Border Collie, running around?"

Everyone shook their head. How could no one see two dogs running footloose and fancy-free?

I returned home exhausted. I hadn't been back long, however, when the phone rang. I picked up the phone and heard a voice, "This is Alachua County Animal Control. Are you missing a Border Collie?"

"Yes. Do you have him?"

"Yes, ma'am. Some students discovered your dog wandering around the halls of Buchholz High School."

"What?" I couldn't have heard that right.

"Your dog was inside Buchholz High School."

"He was found inside the school?"

"Yes, ma'am."

I guess Sirius decided he wanted an education. Only a stupid dog would do that.

"Was there another dog with him?" I asked. "A Jack Russell."

"No, ma'am."

Relief flooded me that I had one dog back. The collar had helped to reunite Sirius with me, but Molly wasn't wearing a collar. She lost it in the yard somewhere, and I never found it. She hated wearing it and would figure out how to get it off, so I didn't buy her a new one.

Immediately, I got back into my car and went to the pound to claim my missing dog. As I drove, I prayed that God would bring Molly back also.

I entered the "holding cell" for homeless dogs with Sirius's blue leash and introduced myself to the desk volunteer. She handed me papers to fill out, and I gave her my credit card.

"Next time the fee is higher," the woman said.

What made her think there would be another time? Of course, Molly was still missing.

The phone rang, and I heard her say something about a Jack Russell.

I tried to get the woman's attention. "Did the person on the line find a Jack Russell?" I asked. "I'm also missing my Jack Russell, Molly."

The woman talked for another minute, and I was about ready to climb over the desk and snatch the phone. Why was she taking so long to answer my question?

Finally, she replied, "A woman found a Jack Russell on 16th Street. She took the dog to the vet, and they scanned her for a microchip. They found one, but they can't get a hold of the owner."

"What's the name?" I asked.

She said the name, and I recognized it as the puppy mill from whom we bought Molly.

"That's my dog. Ask her where she lives, and I'll get her as soon as I take Sirius home."

The volunteer wrote down the address and handed it to me. Just then, Sirius trotted out, holding his head high, as if he were Pharaoh.

I could see it now—all those high school kids making a fuss over him. I could tell it went to his brain. When he saw me, his face brightened up like, "Oh, you found me. I'm ready to go home now."

I was so thrilled to have him back, how could I be mad at him? We left the pound, and I took him home and put him in the yard, making sure I latched the gate. I still didn't know how they'd gotten out. Then I went to pick up Molly.

The woman met me in front of her house. At first, Molly didn't recognize me. (Sight in her one good eye worsened as she grew older.) It took her a second, and for a brief moment, I thought it wasn't Molly, but that was only momentary, long enough for my heart to skip a beat. Then Molly acted like her old self, although quite exhausted. She was too old to be doing such mindless things.

The road where the woman found her was a major thoroughfare. Shopping centers lined both sides of the street. I'll never know how she crossed 43rd and got that far down 23rd without getting hit by a car.

She had traveled a couple of miles farther than Sirius. I supposed when Sirius went to school, Molly just kept going.

"I was able to coax your dog into my car," the woman said. "She came easily."

I thanked her and took Molly home. God had heard my prayers and brought Molly and Sirius safely back to me.

The following Christmas, I baked Christmas cookies and took them to Molly's rescuer. I found out the woman was as much of a dog fanatic as me, maybe even more. I was amused. Her house was decorated entirely with dog knickknacks. Little dog figurines covered the tables around the sofa and chair. She had dog trinkets, dog pillows, and even a children's dog collection. Dog paintings lined the walls.

God had looked out for Molly. The woman who found her was a doggy angel disguised to look like a human. Molly probably would have gotten hit by a car if it had not been for her guardian angel.

31
SIRIUS' GUARDIAN ANGEL

Sirius had a doggie angel, too. He got out of the yard one other time—and considering what an escape artist he was, I'm thankful he had a doggie angel to keep watch over him. I have to admit, I don't know that dogs have doggie angels, but the Lord knew my dog needed one.

Fortunately, Molly had her wits about her this time. She'd had enough adventures in her life. I saw Sirius running up the road as Molly trotted toward the house. Whatever plans I had for the day were kaput. How did they escape? At least Molly thought better of following Sirius and came back on her own.

Since I didn't know how they had gotten loose, I put Molly in her crate. I wanted to check the fencing before I put her in the yard. I quickly scanned the fence, but I didn't see any broken latches, open doors, or holes dug.

I grabbed my keys and drove through the neighborhood, leaning out the window and calling his name. When I didn't see him, I started combing the subdivisions near us. If I saw anybody, I'd ask if they had seen a black and white Border Collie.

I drove around for over an hour, but I had a television show coming up. What was I going to do? By the time I got off the air, it would be dark. Could he find his way back?

I returned home, distracted, and upset. That doesn't make for good focus when captioning. I put Molly out in the backyard to see if she would show me how she and Sirius got out. As soon as I opened the door, Sirius came running up to me. How did he get back in the yard?

I asked my neighbors if they had returned him. Or if they saw someone bring him to my house, but nobody knew anything. To this day, I don't know how Sirius came home. Once again, God sent an angelic friend to help me.

Molly lived to the ripe old age of sixteen. When the night came that we needed to put her to sleep because of cancer, we took her over to Sirius as he lay in his crate to say goodbye.

I don't know if dogs have a sense of death, but I know they have a sense of loss. We knew Sirius would outlive Molly because our delightful Jack Russell was nine when we got Sirius.

For seven years, they romped together in the backyard burying bones that I'm still discovering. I recently found the collar Molly lost under a bunch of decaying leaves. When I shook off the dirt, it appeared she had chewed it in half. She just didn't like wearing a collar.

NEXT K-9 UP

Despite Sirius' fear of that *Star Wars* poster, he proved me wrong about being a coward. One night we were in the living room, and Sirius sprang up to his feet and ran into the sunroom. He'd never behaved so strangely. Was there someone in the backyard?

I peered behind one of the closed window blinds and saw a shadowy figure. Then a sudden burst of light flashed through the blinds.

Now I was spooked. My daughter followed me into the sunroom. I told her to get back. I peeked behind the blind again and saw a large man holding a very bright flashlight, and as my eyes adjusted, I realized he was a cop, and he had a K-9 dog with him.

I was relieved to know it wasn't a burglar, but I was concerned to see a police officer and a German Shepherd. I opened the French door —one of my dumb blonde moments, but I wanted to know what they were doing back there.

The police officer shouted, "Get back in the house, and don't come out."

I hollered back, "If you're looking for someone, a good hiding place is under the pool deck."

"Okay. Now get back in the house."

I closed the door and locked it.

A pounding on the front door followed. I ran into the living room, looked through the blinds, and saw another police officer. I didn't realize that cops had surrounded my house. Then I noticed a dozen patrol cars filled the street.

The officer said, "Whatever you do, don't come outside."

I guess the cop relayed that a dumb blonde had come outside to investigate. I closed the door, sat on the sofa, and waited. Sirius was beside himself. He knew something big was up, and he wasn't sitting in the corner with his tail between his legs. My Border Collie acted like he was next K-9 up if needed.

Soon a fire truck arrived and more police cars. It wasn't long before we heard a helicopter whizzing overhead. Sirens blared as red and blue flashing lights lit up my front yard like Christmas. I'd never been in the middle of a takedown.

The cops spent a lot of time in my backyard. Part of my yard is like a jungle, and I could see the floodlights and hear the officers scurrying around in the woods. Somebody could easily hide out there. My lot abutted a house behind me. Maybe the suspect ran through their yard, jumped the fence, and came into mine.

Soon, all the action shifted from my yard to the property across the street. The house had been vacant for a while and was for sale. Did the person break into that house? I watched as the cop with the K-9 circled the structure several times. They seemed to be at a dead end.

Then a scuffle of activity followed with police officers shouting and the K-9 in pursuit, but I couldn't see well enough in the dark to know what happened.

A few minutes later, a man lay on the ground, surrounded by the cops. They'd caught their prey—with the dog's help. I could go to bed and have sweet dreams.

I never found out what the man did, just that he had escaped from a nearby prison. The real mystery was why the dog kept circling the house. The police officer later told me. The escaped inmate had climbed on top of the roof, and the dog had lost the scent.

Before the officers left, one of them rang my doorbell. I jumped up and ran to open the door. The cop said, "The area is secure. We have the man in custody."

I asked him why the criminal was in my backyard, and he said the convict had cut himself, and the dog was following the blood trail. He jumped over the fence, came through my backyard, and ran across the street to the vacant house.

I thanked the police officer and watched for another hour as all the police cars left, one by one. That was the most exciting event here in decades—except for one other thing that came pretty close. Molly and Sirius made their debut on national television.

FAMOUS DOG STARS

If you read *Children of Dreams*, I talk about neurocysticercosis. After the book was published, I posted a piece on my blog about my daughter's medical condition. The producers of *Monsters Inside Me* on Discovery Channel came across my blog and contacted me. They wanted to feature my daughter's worm story.

A television crew came down from New York and spent two days in Gainesville. The producers interviewed me, my daughter, and the doctors involved in her care. They also interviewed an infectious disease expert at Yale-New Haven Hospital. We had flown up there for a second opinion.

The night the program aired, some friends came over to watch the episode with us. To my surprise, there were a couple of scenes with Molly and Sirius in the backyard, tails wagging, showing their sweet, loving temperament. I couldn't have been more proud. Looking back, they might have been the highlight of the show.

32
POSSUMS AND MORE

I always knew when a lost turtle needed help—both dogs went bonkers with a unique kind of excitement, like on Christmas morning when you get out of bed, and you can't wait to open that large box underneath the tree. You've spent three weeks shaking it, turning it over, listening for audio clues, and even smelling it.

You've tried to peek through the paper, or maybe even unwrapped it without getting caught—I won't tell any family secrets—that's what a turtle was to Molly and Sirius. The poor creature would disappear inside his shell and hide, and my dogs would bark and rattle his turtle cover as the poor creature hid his head.

Sure enough, I'd go out there and find a reptile with a hump on his back. I'd wrap him in a towel and take him to the retention pond three houses down in hopes he could squeeze underneath the fence to safety. After several episodes of turtle rescues, the creature quit coming into my yard. Did the reptile wise up and stay in his pond or go somewhere else?

One day I was over at my neighbor's house, the one with all the cats, and I asked him what was in that great big fish tank in his living room?

He took me over and proudly showed me his pet turtle. "We found him in the yard, and we kept him."

I was pretty sure that humongous turtle was the one that I'd rescued from my dogs. My neighbor's yard was between the retention pond and my house. I watched the turtle swimming around in his quaint abode. He had no idea what a lucky fellow he was.

Once I had a fifty-gallon fish tank, and their turtle tank was three times that size. I was happy all my rescues had led to a happy turtle living in my neighbor's living room.

However, I was wrong once. I discovered my dogs barking at a possum. The critter had wedged itself underneath the fence. Those marsupials have nasty-looking teeth, and my dogs have no brains, so I brought Molly and Sirius inside until the possum moseyed off to greener pastures.

I used to keep the garage door open at night. Knowing what I know now, I bet all those lumpy gifts on the garage floor were possum poops and not Molly poops. The yucky mounds did seem a little mushy for a dog.

I recently discovered that possums love cat food, and I bet they love dog food. That possum was probably coming over to enjoy a delicious meal of Kibbles, and the bonehead got stuck underneath the fence on his return trip to sleep land.

I made the scientific finding when I began to shut the garage door at night. Unbeknownst to me, I was closing up a fat little possum hiding behind some pegboard. I'd go on spells where I'd have poop every morning in front of the door—mushy, watery poop. Which cat with diarrhea was leaving me presents? After a while, I became suspicious.

My daughter had a friend whose father came over and removed the pegboard from the wall—I was sure I saw some fiery eyes back there —and one very upset but quite well-fed possum let us know his thoughts.

"That's the biggest possum I've ever seen," my possum remover said. It took all three of us to get him out of the garage. I now shut the garage door before it gets dark.

We've had many wild animals to visit the garage. Once, I discovered three raccoons having a party by the cat food. One had his head in the cat's water. No wonder the water was disgusting sometimes. I noted three blissful cats were all tucked in their beds with sweet dreams swirling in their heads. I guess they knew I would refill their bowls, so they were quite content to let those masked bandits gorge themselves.

What happened to instincts? I thought cats would want to protect their territory, especially their food. Perhaps, in retrospect, they had more sense than me. I suppose three raccoons could easily outfox three cats.

On another occasion, I discovered four baby possums in the garage. I always heard possums were dumb. Perhaps the momma possum heard about Gainesville's Safe-Haven Law. After all, I'd adopted two daughters and many orphaned dogs and cats.

For a short time, my daughter fell in love with reptiles. One day she came home with a snake in an aquarium.

"You just make sure that snake stays in your room," I told her.

"Don't worry," she promised.

I worried. How can you not worry when there is a snake in your daughter's bedroom? There's only one thing worse than a snake in your daughter's bedroom, and that's a snake your daughter can't find. That three-foot-long reptile disappeared for three weeks, and then I worried about the snake starving. How long can snakes go without eating?

She eventually found him curled up in her closet somewhere. I never asked where, but soon the snake found another home far, far away—in another galaxy.

One summer, Carolina wrens built their home on a shelf among the washer and dryer cleaning supplies. All day, the momma and the daddy delivered worms to their hungry babies. I had to remember not to close the garage door at night. I didn't want the baby birds starving. After a week, I needed to do laundry, so, very carefully, I moved my supplies to a better location, kind of like roads that get diverted to save one little owl.

A few weeks later, I came home, and the momma bird was teaching her little birdies how to fly. When I entered the garage, I didn't know I was interrupting a critical life lesson. When I saw the momma bird squealing and the baby birds squeaking, I stayed in my car. Mama bird was teaching her three babies how to fly out the door into the vast, blue yonder.

Two baby wrens flew out in short order, but the third baby just flapped his wings and cried. After the mamma's frantic pleas and vocal encouragement, the little wren got his act together and flew away. What patience that momma bird had.

Through the years, the neighborhood has undergone many changes. One area near our house was still natural—until a couple of years ago when a new subdivision sprang up.

One night I was walking Sirius, and we stumbled upon a dozen deer foraging along our street. When they heard me, they took off. I was sad that new houses occupied their small little vestige of natural habitat, and they had no better place to go in search of food.

Years ago, a deer appeared in my backyard. He must have jumped the fence like the convict and made himself at home in the woodsy area of my backyard for a time. My daughter has asked me to clear out that jungle many times, but my answer has always been the same. Wildlife needs a place to go. Soon there won't be any land remaining just for them.

Besides that, I love feeding the birds. By providing natural woodlands, I have more birds at my feeding stations and birdbaths than I would have otherwise.

Every summer, for years, we would have a nesting pair of birds to set up residence in the purple martin house in our backyard, though purple martins never used it. Great crested flycatchers found it and returned year after year.

We knew they had arrived when we heard them in the trees. If they thought I was watching, they would fly away. Toward the end of the summer, when the babies had fledged, squirrels would move in and stay.

Each year when I took the birdhouse down, I'd find one large hole in the middle. The squirrels would always remodel the interior, and the next year, if I didn't get a new birdhouse, the flycatchers would enjoy a mansion.

One spring, I replaced the purple martin house with a bluebird house even though I wasn't sure if we would attract any bluebirds. When I saw a scout a few weeks later, I thought we might get lucky. After all, my property was prime real estate.

I had what I would consider Park Place on a Monopoly board. The birdhouse front faced the canopy of honeysuckles, red tips, cassia, Mexican petunia, and water oak; and a small flower garden including shrimp plants, milkweed, Penta, and large philodendrons surrounded it. My pool rounded out the open area.

Each spring, I would check the birdhouse to see if it needed any repairs. One year, I knew I should buy a new one. The warped base made the house unstable, and only a plastic tie secured it, but I got busy and forgot about it.

The bluebirds arrived and began building their nest. I watched as they carried leaves, moss, and twigs into the hole. A few weeks later, I heard the faint sounds of babies. I was excited once again to watch the back and forth ritual of the parents feeding the babies.

However, when a few days passed, and I hadn't heard or seen them, I became concerned. Had a predator got to them? I looked around my property to make sure I didn't miss a dead bluebird.

I gave up the search when I saw the parents working on the nest again. They appeared to be rebuilding. Perhaps the babies had already "flown the coop."

Several days later, I went out for my daily swim. When I glanced up at the birdhouse, I saw two beady eyes staring out of the dark hole. They were much too big to be bluebird eyes.

Surprised, I examined the front of the birdhouse with binoculars and noticed the hole had been gnawed bigger—large enough for one determined squirrel to squeeze into, though I imagined it was a very tight fit. The occupant peered out of its new home.

It would have been comical if I had not recently seen the birds bringing in nesting material. But what could I do? Distracted, I entered the pool. Was the squirrel sitting on the eggs, or worse, smothering the babies?

After a while, I watched the male and female bluebirds fly over to the bluebird house. At the last minute, they halted their approach in midair and instead perched on a tree. It appeared they had no idea there was a squirrel inside their quarters. I was upset because the squirrel had the entire canopy in which to build her nest.

I climbed out of the pool, grabbed the pole that I used for skimming the water, and angled it up to the birdhouse. The squirrel jumped out like she had been stung by a hornet. Wild eyes flashed as she scrambled past me, jumped from the fence into the thicket, and scurried off faster than a startled fish.

My job accomplished, I dipped back into the pool and swam to the far end. I hoped to see the bluebirds reclaim their territory, but they didn't return. Perhaps they were waiting for me to leave. Darkness was approaching anyway, so I got out, dried off, and went inside.

Then I heard my daughter's frantic scream, "Mamma, the bluebird house fell over."

"What?" I ran out the backdoor. The partially burst open box was lying on the ground. The squirrel broke the plastic tie when he scrambled out of the tiny hole. The destroyed house was beyond repair. Some nesting material had fallen out of the sides where the wooden boards had separated.

I peered through the hole searching for baby birds or eggs, but to my dismay, instead, I saw two baby squirrels. I did a double-take because I expected to see baby birds. They were tiny with no hair and couldn't have been more than a few days old.

Would the mother return? How could the squirrel have been using the house at the same time? The babies didn't appear to be hurt. At least they were moving around as much as baby squirrels do with their eyes still closed.

The nesting debris had cushioned the fall, though I wondered how so much "stuff" could fit into such a small space. We needed to figure out how to put the birdhouse back on the post. The base of it had rotted, and there was nothing to which we could mount it. I managed to force the sides of the box back together.

I set the birdhouse on the table by the pool and went to the garage to find something we could use. My daughter later told me she saw the mother squirrel return and leave. That was a good sign. I hoped that she would come back.

I found a roll of sticky blue tape that we had used to cover the windows during the last hurricane season. We could use a screw to latch it on the post and run the tape around the sides and underneath it. We took turns pulling off tape and wrapping it like a Band-aid. When we finished, nighttime had fallen, and we went back inside to watch.

A bluebird arrived immediately, but he refused to go in. He just sat outside the opening. We got tired of watching the perched bird, and he was in the shadows anyway. I went to bed thinking about baby squirrels and feeling guilty for my part in the disaster. I wondered what I would do if the mother did not return.

The next day I kept an eye out for her, but the birdhouse just baked in the sun with no squirrel to be seen. By late afternoon I had to do something. I took my daughter to the gym and visited a friend who took care of orphaned animals.

I asked her if she would take them if I retrieved the babies. She reassured me she would. I ran home, climbed up on the railing once again, and brought the box down. I set it on the table and looked inside, but to my dismay, the box was empty.

My friend said the mother might have returned that night or early in the morning. She explained that squirrels make several nests, so if ants overran one nest or she was scared off, she had another one to which she could carry her babies.

I still felt sorry for the birds. I went to the store and bought a new bluebird house that a determined squirrel couldn't gnaw through. My neighbor came over later that evening and anchored it so it couldn't get knocked over again. My biggest regret was that I hadn't done it sooner.

But no birds used the new birdhouse that year. It remained empty, much to my disappointment. My letdown was even more significant because the house was expensive, better built, and one the squirrels couldn't destroy.

The next year, I was excited one morning when I walked out on my porch, looked up at the birdhouse, and saw two eyes peering out the round hole. But the eyes looked sketchy. What kind of bird was that? Maybe I just imagined I saw eyes. I needed a better look. I even brought out the binoculars. I could tell they were eyes, but they were the strangest bird eyes I'd ever seen. Whatever species it was, it wasn't a Great Crested Flycatcher or bluebirds.

For three days, I saw those eyes. They never changed. They just stared out of the hole. Could it be a dead bird? If it was, I wanted to remove him so a momma bird could make a nest up there. I'd paid good money for that birdhouse, and I wanted some return on my investment.

I went to the garage to fetch the ladder. I had bought it from QVC while captioning. I watched the guy set it up in fifteen seconds, and he convinced me I could do the same.

It took me a lot longer than fifteen seconds to set up that unwieldy contraption. I put it together backward, where the top was down, and the bottom was up. Where are men when you need one?

Finally, with screwdriver in hand, I placed the ladder against the wooden pole and climbed up.

Once I reached the top, I peered through the small opening, but it was so bright outside and so dark inside, I couldn't see anything but two eyes staring back—not even a blink.

I'd have to unscrew the top to see what kind of bird it was. Twelve feet up, leaning forward against the ladder, I unscrewed the lid. What did I see? A bullfrog perched up against the opening, looking out with those big bulging frog eyes.

I put the lid back on the birdhouse. That frog spent the whole summer in there, except I know he came out at night. One night when I went swimming, I saw him jumping around in the pool with me. I supposed he felt like he had found the best luxury home—a high rise apartment—overlooking Echo Lake.

When the next summer came, I hoped for a bird to claim the house, but the darn frog was back. I saw his eyes again through the hole. That bullfrog spent two years in that birdhouse.

This year, at last, I had a nesting pair of birds—some Carolina wrens. I miss the Great Crested Flycatchers, but I'm glad to have a bird and not a bullfrog taking up residence in the hundred-dollar birdhouse. Of course, I'd love to have some nesting bluebirds—maybe next year.

33
TWILA

I felt like my younger daughter was missing out on all the fun. The other one had raised four cats. I was a dog lover at heart, so I asked her if she would like a dog or a cat for her birthday. Until now, the only animal she'd had was a gerbil.

My daughter was turning eleven, and when she said she wanted a cat, I was excited. I told her I would take her to the Humane Society to pick out her very own kitten.

"I won't go to the dog dormitory," I promised her. "I'm going with you to the cat motel."

Because I'd wised up in my old age, I knew I had to stay away from the dog kennels. It would be like me to fall in love with another dog that looked like Shelley and bring home a dog and a cat.

We hopped in my trusty green Sienna once again and took a short trip to the animal homeless shelter. We went straight to the kitten area—no detours—and one tiny, all-gray kitten caught my daughter's attention.

The volunteer pulled the kitty out, and my daughter stroked the tiny feline's head. They seemed to hit it off, and I hoped this little kitten would bring my birthday daughter lots of happiness.

I signed all the paperwork and paid the adoption fee to adopt Twila—the perfect name for an all-gray cat—and we climbed into the van to return home. I was delighted this time we were bringing back only one animal and not two. Sirius was terrific when he wasn't a bad dog, but I didn't want another dog.

I pulled out onto 6th Street and hit the red light to turn west on N.W. 39th Avenue.

The light turned green, and I made a left turn, happy as a schoolgirl on the last day of school. Seconds later, I see a police car behind me with a swirling blue and red light.

"A cop just stopped me," I told my daughter. "I need to pull off on the road here."

I didn't think I was speeding, and my tag wasn't expired, so I couldn't imagine why she stopped me.

After I parked, the dutiful policewoman came up to my side window. "Can I see your driver's license?"

I dug through my purse and handed it to her.

"Did you know you were going thirty-two miles per hour in a fifteen-mile-per-hour school zone?"

"The speed limit is fifteen?" I asked. I looked around for a speed limit sign.

Her eyes bore into me with annoying superiority. I never liked women police officers. They always give you a ticket even when you aren't speeding.

"When the light is blinking," she said. "This is a school zone."

As she said the words, I saw the blinking lights for the first time.

"They must have started blinking when I sat at the red light," I protested. "They weren't blinking when I pulled out onto 6th Street."

I pointed to the back seat. "We just came from the Humane Society. Today is my daughter's birthday, and we adopted a kitten."

The female cop could have cared less and continued to write up a ticket. She stepped back to the police car, probably to run my driver's license.

When I looked back in my review mirror, I saw my birthday daughter texting her big sister with too much exuberance. I bit my lip. How much was this going to cost?

The cop reappeared, handed me a yellow slip of paper, and returned my driver's license. As she walked away, I looked at the ticket—$450! I nearly croaked. If the light hadn't been blinking, I wouldn't have been speeding.

What should have been a delightful birthday present for my daughter turned into an expensive Humane Society adoption visit. I did the best I could to forget about it. We brought Twila home and began introducing her to the other animals.

The next morning, I went to check on my daughter's new kitten, and to my dismay, Twila's left eye was twice the size it should have been. It looked like it was protruding so far out that it would fall out of the socket.

My daughter was horrified, so much so I could read on her face what she was thinking. I don't want that kitten anymore. She's ugly and deformed like a monster from *The Twilight Zone.*

I immediately took Twila to the vet to have her eye checked. As it turned out, it looked worse than it was.

"Give Twila this antibiotic," the vet said, "and she should be fine in a few days."

"Her eye will go back to normal?"

The vet assured me that it would. I went home feeling relieved. "I'll believe it when I see it," I said to myself.

Between the speeding ticket and Twila's deformed eye, I was beginning to think we'd made a mistake, but I still had hope. If we didn't adopt her, who would? Nobody would want a cat that looked like a monster. Even Molly, with only one functioning eye, didn't look grotesque.

I came home and shared the good news with my daughter. Within a few days, the swelling went down, and after a week, her eye was normal again.

Timing is everything. Twila must have developed an infection in the eye before we adopted her, but it didn't become visible until we took her home. The Lord meant for the sweet feline to be ours.

We still have Twila a decade later. After being an inside–outside cat for several years, we made her an outside cat when she became afraid of the ceiling fans. She was so afraid she didn't want to come out from underneath my bed. I've been slowly bringing her back inside to acclimate her again. After a spectacular arrival, she lives a quiet life—predictable and constant. In many ways, she's still the baby we adopted. She only weighs seven pounds.

34
LEWIS AND JAMES

When we adopted Lily and Sirius, one of my daughters learned about the fostering program at the Alachua County Humane Society. The program allows the Humane Society to board more dogs and cats, and the foster families learn about the animals in their care.

The families socialize the future adoptees, get to know their personalities, and the foster families pass that valuable information along to the Humane Society and hopeful adopters.

I wasn't surprised when my daughter approached me about

fostering cats. I wasn't totally against it, but I can't say I was totally for it either. But I didn't want to deny her the opportunity as long as I didn't have to do any of the work—I already had plenty to do—and since my daughter could drive now, she could fulfill all the obligations that fostering entailed.

As I weighed the pros and cons, I concluded it would be good to allow her to give back to the community. How many teens are willing to foster animals? It requires commitment and sacrifice. The Humane Society had made great strides getting away from euthanizing so many unwanted pets. If they had more volunteers to foster, perhaps hundreds more dogs and cats could be saved.

Of course, my greatest fear was my daughter would want to keep the cats.

"We can't keep them," I told her. "You have to return the cats to the Humane Society when the time is up so they can be adopted."

"I'll do that," she promised.

Later that week, she returned home with two kittens, a strikingly marked orange taffy and an all-black, puny-looking cat. Supposedly they were litter mates, but they looked nothing like each other.

When the time came to return them to the Humane Society, she was willing to give them up. I wasn't.

Lewis

Lewis, as we named him, was an exceptional cat. He had the distinct coloring of a wild African lion, and he was one of the sweetest cats we'd had the joy of owning. James, on the other hand, was black and awkward. He wasn't beautiful like his brother.

My daughters loved Lewis because he was easy to love. James wasn't as easy to love, so I loved him more. I wanted to make him as sweet as Lewis.

One of my daughters had become a level seven gymnast, and we were traveling around the country to various competitions. We had a gym meet in San Antonio, Texas. I kept James in the house while we were gone and kept the other cats outside. We had a house sitter to take care of them and our two dogs. We had too many cats and dogs to board now; I preferred to have a house sitter come and stay.

We returned home from a successful gymnastics meet, and I asked the house sitter about the animals.

"I haven't seen Lewis in a couple of days," she said.

I put up signs, scoured the neighborhood, and cried. Why didn't I keep Lewis inside with James? As it turned out, James didn't like being alone in the house. Or maybe he didn't like the cat sitter.

He peed all over the kitchen countertop. I must have spent three hours cleaning that area. I should have kept Lewis inside the house with him. That would have kept Lewis safe, and James might not have been a bad cat while we were gone.

After that, I put James out of the house. I still loved him, but I couldn't be worried about him doing it again. Even the thought of him getting on the countertop where I prepared food and cooked was unsettling.

A week later, I attended the Florida Christian Writer's Conference to present my adoption memoir *Children of Dreams* to several agents and publishers. I came home depressed.

I remember that week like it was yesterday. Guilt plagued me that Lewis was missing. One of my biggest fears was somebody would steal him. He was affectionate and stunningly beautiful. I like to think somebody took him and gave him a loving home.

All these years later, he lives in my heart even if he's not physically with us. I can still see Lewis zipping across the yard as I would stop and admire his beauty. He was that exotic-looking.

I heard a woman exclaim once over the radio, "You guys cry over losing your dog, but losing a cat is just as hard."

I didn't have cats back when I heard the woman say that, but she was right. I don't know if you ever get over losing an animal, especially when they disappear unexpectedly. There isn't the closure, and you think perhaps he or she might return. I've never given up hope that Lewis will show up one day. You hear about those kinds of miraculous reunions.

We still have James, who is eleven. After all these years, he's still not allowed in the house. We've tried to bring him inside a few times, to make him an indoor–outdoor cat, but he has a spraying issue. Why some cats feel like they need to mark their territory and others don't, I don't know.

As I work in my garden, he always comes over and keeps me company, and I love petting him and listening to him purr. He's my faithful garden companion.

Over the next four years following Lewis's disappearance, things didn't seem the same in the Roberts' household without an orange tabby cat lounging on my bed. The hurt cut deep in all of us.

One day I was captioning, and I received an urgent phone call from my daughter. I could always tell by the first word out of her mouth if something was up.

35
ANAKIN

"Mother, there is a beautiful orange kitten that looks like Lewis at the flea market …" She didn't need to finish the sentence.

"Bring him home."

I felt like God was saying, "You've grieved long enough."

My daughter and some friends had gone to a flea market, and one of them heard what sounded like kittens meowing. They followed the cries and discovered four babies.

Less than an hour later, my daughter rushed into my bedroom with a tiny kitten—so small that my hand swallowed him up. I wondered what happened to his mother. Without intervention, he'd never have survived. He was too small, and I was kitten-smitten.

At first, the timid orange bundle of fur barely moved. I gently rubbed the little fellow with my fingertip, massaged behind the ears, and petted him on the head. As the kitten was mesmerized by my kindness, his fear evaporated.

With a little coaxing, he rolled over on his back and exposed his belly, a sign of trust. Being so young, not having lived long enough to be hurt, he quickly bonded with us. I'd made a new friend for life.

The mother had abandoned the kittens in the woods, and the flea market was giving them away. My cat daughter named the orange cat Anakin. To say I was thrilled to have another orange cat is an understatement.

He wasn't as spectacular as Lewis with deep mackerel markings, but Anakin had light tiger stripes on his legs and back with a crinkly "M" on his forehead. He was also sweet, like Lewis. Our hearts were full again with an orange tabby.

While no cat could replace Lewis, I believe God knew we needed an orange cat. No other color would do. He had to be orange, and in four years, we had not come across any orange cats needing a home.

I remember one evening Anakin climbed inside my scuba diving wetsuit. I imagine it was nice and warm in there; it sure kept me warm when diving in cold water. How many kittens get to enjoy the inside of a warm wetsuit?

Anakin is a high-strung cat. If I change the furniture around, he gets paranoid. If someone comes to the house that he doesn't know, he hides. To those he loves, he is affectionate and loyal. Without his calming collar, he becomes a scaredy-cat.

Many times we've had to be a cat psychologist with Anakin. He is complicated. Where is a real cat psychologist when you need one?

There is a downside to having more than one cat. Cats can become territorial, and we soon discovered we had cat markings where they ought not to be. How could I know which cat was the culprit? We eventually made Boots, James, Lily, and Twila outdoor cats. Anakin we kept inside.

Fortunately, we have a large lot, and much of it is still natural. It would be interesting to know how many lizards make their home on our property. More than once, one of our cats has blessed us with a lizard present on the front porch. And we have plenty of flying roaches in the trees and other things that hop, jump, sting, buzz, crawl, and annoy us.

Rarely, one of the cats would catch a bird. Fortunately, they've never been very good at bird-napping, and we've been able to rescue most of them—even a bird we discovered on the sidewalk by our front door.

Instead of going to church one Sunday for Easter, we took the injured bird to a local sanctuary near Ocala. We later learned the shelter released him as good as new. I've tried to think of a spiritual message to tie into Easter. I'm still thinking.

Sometimes critters would even get inside the house. One evening after I went to bed, I heard a loud disturbance in the other room. A cat that shall remain anonymous was running around in the living room with a cicada in his mouth—you know, those ugly insects that sing in a high-pitched vibration to woo a mate?

I don't know how that bug thought he'd find a mate in my cat's mouth, but I had one upset cat on my hands. The hapless feline couldn't get the unfortunate victim dislodged. After much consternation and a frantic prayer, the singing wannabe lover fell onto the living room floor.

I quickly grabbed the terrified romantic and dumped him outside in the bushes. One relieved but embarrassed feline rubbed up against my leg. I had come to the rescue once more.

Not only do cats have nine lives, they never sleep. I would know. They are wont to chase invisible enemies. One night Anakin woke me up. When I opened my eyes, I saw him swiping at something dark. I didn't know what it was, but instinctively, I swung at it, too, shooing it away.

Suddenly, a mysterious winged creature flew out of my bedroom. I had no fear and just went back to sleep. Jesus was my protector.

Since we didn't know what happened to Lewis, we were reluctant to let Anakin outdoors. Maybe orange cats are more visible to predators. I still think someone stole Lewis, but because I've yet to see orange grass (even though we have orange trees), an orange tabby might be easier to spot than a black or white cat.

The few times Anakin has stepped out of the house has resulted in him immediately running back inside. His paranoia makes him a homebody. Then, my daughter got the idea (the second time she got this original idea) that she wanted to foster kittens again.

36
KENOBI

I had reservations this time about fostering. We failed the last time my daughter fostered because we kept both kittens. I didn't want any more animals. With all the dog food and cat food and checkups and vaccinations and pet care when we went out of town, my animal expenses were high.

My daughter understood, and so I said okay. A few days later, she came home with not one or two kittens, not three or four kittens, but five kittens and a momma cat—six cats in all.

My daughter set up the crate in her bedroom and put the momma cat in it with her babies. Thank goodness we had such a large container since it was such a large family.

"Is the momma cat nice?" I asked my daughter. I didn't want to think about her getting scratched. She had had cat scratch fever when she was younger.

I had that overwhelming sense—to use the proverbial phrase—that she had bit off more than she could chew. How was she going to take care of all these cats? I also knew she was a light sleeper. Was she going to be able to sleep with six cats just a few feet from her bed?

Plus, the momma cat was quite a mess. Her coat was in poor condition, and she was filthy.

"Momma cat is sweet," my daughter said.

I watched as she set everything up. Once everything was in place, my daughter put all the cats in the crate. The kittens were too small to be separated from their mother. Feeding time had arrived.

My daughter looked exhausted—a happy kind of exhaustion.

"Do they have many foster families that take in five cats and a momma cat?"

"This was the biggest litter," she said. "I didn't put a limit on how many I would take. Some families only take one or two kittens."

I leaned over and peered into the crate as the babies kneaded on their momma's belly drinking milk from her nipples. I could hear sweet little purring sounds. The tranquility of it touched me, reflecting contentment to the Nth degree.

A few years earlier, without the fostering program, the momma cat for sure and possibly even her babies would have been euthanized.

I was proud of my daughter for taking on such an overwhelming job. It's not as mindless or as easy as it seems because the cats must be taken to the Humane Society for deworming, shots, spaying, neutering, and any illness that comes up—and foster animals usually come with complex issues. The Humane Society rescued them from somewhere. Sometimes animals are near starvation when brought in. Other times, they are filled with fright or injured or too sick to be saved.

As all these thoughts filled my mind, I could tell my daughter was ready for me to leave.

"You can look at them tomorrow," she said. "I need to get some sleep."

I didn't see much of them for the next couple of days. Then my daughter decided to bathe the momma cat.

"She's just too dirty," she said.

That went about as well as could be expected, no doubt the cat's first bath, but Momma cat looked spiffier the next time I saw her. She was mostly black with some white on her face. From what I could tell, she was a good mother. She'd lie there and let her babies feed for as long as it took. I'd watch for a few minutes between captioning shows. We kept them separated from the rest of the cats because we didn't want our cats to pick up any parasites they might have.

After a few days, my daughter said she wasn't getting enough rest. Everybody knows cats don't sleep through the night. They have nine lives. We moved the babies and the momma cat into the bathroom. That lasted for a while.

I hadn't had much interaction with the babies, keeping my distance, knowing we couldn't keep them, but as the kittens grew, it became harder to manage them properly in the bathroom.

Then my daughter asked if we could put them in the kitchen. We put up a partition at the kitchen entrance, ensuring we kept the foster cats away from our cats. Now that the babies had undergone several hand-washings, plus all the socializing my daughter did to prepare them for adoption by a forever family, they were adorable, eye-catching, attention-grabbing kittens. I could hardly walk past them without stopping to pick up one.

One was brown and white, one was black, one was gray, and two were black and white. The kittens stayed in the kitchen, and I would prepare meals being careful where I stepped. Now that I was around them more, I started to become acquainted with them. The days passed, and as they quickly grew, I knew the time was coming when my daughter would have to return them.

One of the black and white kittens stood out above all the others.

His head was black with a white point on his nose between his eyes as if he wore a mask. The fluffy white fur on his chest extended down his legs to his paws. His coat was like soft velvet. He was stunningly beautiful, but his personality was what stood out from the rest of his littermates.

He walked around, holding his head high and his tail tall, asserting his dominance over the litter. He had a mighty warrior's self-assurance and the heart of a gentle giant. He purred constantly and always wanted to be with my daughter or me.

By now, we'd been around lots of cats, adopted many cats, rescued several cats, fostered a bunch of cats, and knew all about cats. This kitten was special. He was in a category of his own.

I lamented the coming day when we would have to say goodbye. I wrestled with it, part of me wishing we hadn't fostered them. My daughter had done ninety-five percent of the work, but I couldn't go into the kitchen and not pet the kittens or play with them for a few minutes. And my eyes were always on that one special black and white kitten.

The annual adoption fair was approaching when families would adopt many dogs and cats. The money raised at the event would help to support the Humane Society throughout the coming year. We had five kittens and a momma cat the Humane Society would be eager to feature at their adoption show.

I was in my bedroom when my daughter came in and sat on my bed. She was quiet for a moment, hesitant. I waited for her to say something.

"I know you said we couldn't keep any of them," she said, "but could we keep just one."

I focused on my daughter, her brown eyes pleading with me, hopeful yet resigned that I'd say no. She knew she had to keep her word to me, but now that she was parting with them, I could feel her overwhelming sadness.

"I wonder if it's the same one I want to keep," I said. I didn't know how to describe which one it was. I just knew the kitten when I saw him.

I hadn't shared my feelings with my daughter. I felt like I needed to set an example. How could I expect her to respect my wishes if I kept one kitten for myself?

"Is it the one with the circle on his right shoulder?" she asked me.

I didn't know. I'd never win the award for the most observant person in the world. I just knew which kitten had smitten me with cat love.

I got up from my desk and walked into the kitchen and pointed. "It's that one."

"That's the same one I want to keep," she said.

So out of five kittens, we had both fallen in love with the same one. What were the chances of that? It wasn't that he was more beautiful than the others, but something about him was special. In that instant, I knew we had to keep him.

37
FAYE

I felt ten pounds lighter—and that's a good feeling when I can't lose one measly pound. In one fell swoop, joy surprised me.

While I was sad to see Momma cat and her four kittens depart, I knew we'd socialized them and they would all make lovable family pets. We'd poured our hearts into them, especially the kittens. Momma cat had been very tolerant of us with our constant intrusion. I think she liked the break from her mothering duties when the kittens played with us.

The big day arrived. My daughter carted off Momma cat and her four kittens, and we went through the formal adoption of Kenobi. The big adoption event was the upcoming weekend, so the Humane Society was anxious to receive the kittens, cats, puppies, and dogs from the foster families.

I said goodbye to the four remaining kittens and Momma cat. Of course, transporting the animals is stressful for the animals, but this final goodbye stressed me more. I comforted myself that I'd stop by the Humane Society on Sunday. I wanted Momma cat to get adopted quickly. Kittens find homes swiftly, but adult dogs and cats take longer.

On Sunday afternoon, I drove to the Humane Society with mixed emotions. I wanted Momma cat and her babies to be gone, but I also wanted to see them.

When I arrived, there were only a handful of visitors. I went from room to room, checking out the cats and kittens remaining. I was sad to see so many. I was surprised to see a couple of Momma cat's kittens; only two had found homes. The remaining two would have to wait. If only more people would adopt animals. I learned later almost a hundred dogs and cats found forever homes that weekend.

I didn't see Momma cat. Kittens get adopted first, and not to see Momma cat made me think someone chose her. I asked the volunteer about Momma cat. The Humane Society had named her Faye. She didn't remember a cat named Faye being adopted.

The Humane Society worker went through the list of dogs and cats that they had placed that weekend, but Faye's name wasn't on the list. I went back and checked again. Momma cat wasn't in any of the holding pens.

"I don't know where she is," the volunteer said. "Are you sure you have the right name?"

I told her we had fostered her, and I was sure her name was Faye. She checked their records and saw that we had taken care of a Momma cat by the name of Faye with five kittens. The volunteer shook her head. "I don't know where she is. That's very odd."

"You wouldn't have put her down?" I asked.

The volunteer shook her head. "No, we wouldn't have done that." She looked at me, blankly.

I turned away. Something must have happened, but what?

The next day I received a call from the Humane Society. The woman said, "Are you the family that fostered Faye and five baby kittens?"

I assured her that we were.

The woman continued. "Faye had an accident and injured herself. We took her to the vet to have surgery, and until she's healed, she's not adoptable. Would you be interested in fostering her again while she recovers?"

Without a moment's hesitation, I said, "Yes."

She said she would get back to me when they received her from the vet.

FAYE COMES HOME

The next day I went to pick up Momma cat. "Faye doesn't like to be in a crate," the Humane Society volunteer said. "She tried to get out of the crate and got her paw caught in the bar. The vet had to remove one of her claws."

Faye's leg was bandaged, and she wore a collar. She was one unhappy Momma cat, but she perked up when we brought her home. She was glad to see one of her kittens, Kenobi.

Her recovery went quickly, and fortunately, there was no nerve damage. She had a normal gait when walking. That would make her more adoptable, but there was one problem. I had fallen in love with her. Seeing her suffer through such a painful injury and then make a full recovery was heart-warming.

Ten days later, the Humane Society wanted me to bring her back so a forever family could adopt her.

"I wish I could keep her, but I can't," I said to the volunteer. "We already have seven—six cats and a dog."

I dropped Faye off and wrestled all the way home with leaving her. How could I do this? I twisted and turned all night. The next morning, I called the Humane Society.

"I want to adopt Faye," I told them. "Can I have her back?"

The volunteer questioned me. "Are you sure? You said you already had seven animals and couldn't afford to keep her?"

"I know," I replied. "But I made a mistake. I realize now that I love Faye, and I don't want to part with her."

After more discussion, she asked me to wait two days and see how I felt. Two days later, I called the Humane Society. "I still want to adopt Faye."

I drove over, filled out the paperwork, and brought Momma cat home. Faye is the last cat we adopted —seven years ago.

We soon discovered she was the most obedient out of all our animals. I think she knew how lucky she was to have found a home. The first couple of years of her life were hard: She'd been a mother out of wedlock, five babies to take care of, with barely enough food for herself. Now she lived a care-free life, lounging on the chair all day beside her human savior, eating and getting fat. She was one happy, well-behaved cat.

38
ONE HAPPY FAMILY

Faye made the house feel full again. A little introspection can prompt deep thoughts. Was I that old woman who lived in the shoe who had so many cats she didn't know what to do?

Of course not! I wasn't old, and I had plenty to do. I loved the sounds of yelping dogs and cats that purred. I reveled in wagging tails and balls of fur.

Despite having to explain to anyone who asked how we ended up with seven cats and a dog, my Father was in it. God doesn't count things the same way we do. Sacrificial love never calculates the cost. We find contentment in those things that bring us joy. And our highest satisfaction comes when we know that God's will is in it.

To love once-homeless dogs and cats filled our hearts, and it didn't take long for all our delightful pets to find their bailiwick. Each brought us joy and touched our lives. They were four-legged companions with unique personalities, passions, and quirky habits.

I thought about Lily. She brought my teenage daughter, a cat foster hero, a cheerful heart that grew her into a responsible young woman. The tiny bundle of fur blossomed into a loyal companion. The bond between them will be eternal, just like my bond with my childhood pet, Gypsy.

Lily considered me her butler. At her insistence, I'd let her in and out of the house or into my daughter's bedroom. I'm not even sure she knew my name.

Sirius, my Border Collie, was a delightful mix of wildness and sweetness. He knew my name all too well. He loved everybody and everything, but he loved me the most.

Early on, Sirius was Molly's keeper, and in his later years, he spent most of his time inside because of allergies. He herded Kenobi with great delight and enjoyed long siestas on his luxurious pillow a few feet from my captioning chair.

Twila, my daughter's all-gray cat, came wrapped as a $600 birthday present because of my $450 speeding ticket; and her sweet buddy, James, is always near.

Twila never grew up. She stayed small, spunky, and insecure. However, the seven-pound feline can take care of herself—thank you very much—to the surprise of veterinarians who still underestimate her grittiness when they administer any treatment to her.

Boots found contentment wherever he was and was low maintenance. As a solitary creature, he had his favorite hideouts, like underneath the philodendrons in the back, on a heated blanket in the garage, or I'd catch him snoozing in the front yard by the flowers. He was a loner.

As he got older, he developed arthritis, but even that didn't curtail his contentment and appreciation of everything we did to make his senior life easier. We eventually brought him inside and he became an indoor cat, much to his delight. His typical day consists of going from one resting place to another.

Tinkerbell rehomed herself. I was sad the day she told me she was going to less crowded pastures, but she had been leaving us little by little.

I vividly remember the day she said farewell. "I've found a home where there aren't as many cats, and I'd rather live there instead of here. But I still love you, and thank you for rescuing me."

Anakin brought us joy from the first day he arrived. While Anakin didn't care much for Momma cat, he loved Kenobi. Anakin was only a year older than Kenobi, so the two were close in age and inseparable.

One of Anakin's and Kenobi's favorite places was on my bed. Whether I was captioning or writing a book, they were near. And they would entertain me as they groomed each other and carried on endless cat conversations.

They could be catnapping on the sofa, hunting lizards on the porch, or sun tanning through the skylights, where one was, the other was, too. They stuck closer than brothers.

Many nights, my felines would shut-eye with me. Sometimes, though, I needed my space and insisted they sleep in the living room. As soon as I opened my door the next morning, they would scamper in for their morning hugs and head pats. I'd be treated to whimsical purrs as they told me how much they loved me.

One day, Kenobi did something I didn't like. I don't remember what it was, but I was disgruntled enough that I put him outside. There he sat, staring at the closed front door.

Feeling bad, I brought him back inside, and he never went out again—except on the screened-in porch to watch birds and catch unsuspecting lizards. I learned that day how much Kenobi loved us. He wasn't willing to move an inch from the front door.

James took up temporary residence for a while with our neighbor and became their foster child until their son was born. Then he realized we were his favorite home. When I began gardening again, James wanted to be with me. During my quiet time on the bench, he sits with me. He's my faithful garden companion.

One day, I dashed through the living room, and as I stepped over Sirius, he got up, sending me crashing to the floor. I landed on the runner and wasn't hurt, but it reminded me of the passing of years. I took my time getting up. You know you have fewer years in front of you when you trip over the dog, and your daughter brings you ginger tea.

Despite an occasional territorial spat, we were one happy family. Even the animals learned to be tolerant of the other four-legged family members. I let them know if I wasn't pleased with their behavior. Do animals test us? I believe they do, just like children. They need boundaries; yet, they also want reassurance they are loved.

The first week after I adopted Faye, she peed on my bed. I think she was testing me to see if I'd take her back to the Humane Society. The queen quilt she soiled was large and heavy, too big for our washer and dryer. So I took it to the cleaners to use theirs. Washing it was easy; drying it was another matter. Others brought in their laundry and left. I just kept putting in more quarters.

Sometimes, the way things happen, I know it's not by chance, especially with cats. They are complicated creatures and solitary by nature.

God is the animal keeper, and if there were a thousand cats on a hill and ten thousand dogs on a mountain, God would know the names of each one of them. I find that reassuring and comforting.

We'd had many cats by the time we adopted Faye, and while we loved them all, Kenobi had a special place in our hearts. He was so sweet, so affectionate, so...perfect... until the accident, and then his young life at two was turned upside down.

39
KENOBI'S ACCIDENT

One day, my daughter was vacuuming the living room. She's much better at cleaning than me, pulling out sofas and chairs and moving furniture to get into the corners. As I walked from my bedroom to the kitchen, I caught Kenobi streaking like lightning across the living room. He ran so fast from the vacuum cleaner I could hardly tell that it was him.

I didn't think much more about it at the time, until later in the day when it occurred to me I hadn't seen him for a few hours. That was highly unusual because he was always with somebody, usually me.

I looked behind the sofa, but he wasn't there. I called for him, and when he didn't appear, I went outside to see if he had wandered off. I couldn't imagine he would venture out.

I became increasingly concerned. Where was Kenobi? My daughter said she remembered seeing something white behind her when she was vacuuming—just as I had seen. She joined in the search to find him.

Five hours passed, and our search intensified. I started moving furniture around. When I pulled the sofa away from the wall, he popped out. The poor fellow must have gotten trapped underneath the couch. Our excitement dissipated when we watched him limp to his litter box, groaning in great distress.

That night, Kenobi rested in a corner on a rug with his hip propped up. I noticed he was breathing heavily, but when I approached him, he hissed. He felt feverish, and the next day I took him to the vet. X-rays revealed he had broken both hips.

The vet prescribed some pain medicine, and we elected to try the conservative approach first—bed rest for two months in a crate. Follow up X-rays revealed his hips had not healed, and the left hip was more displaced than before. He didn't appear to be in as much pain, but he walked with a noticeable limp and couldn't run or jump on the sofa or bed.

The right hip didn't seem symptomatic, so the vet recommended we just do surgery on the left hip, but there was another problem. He had a heart murmur. Whoever heard of a two-year-old cat having a heart murmur? Surely that couldn't be anything serious.

Our vet recommended we take Kenobi to The University of Florida Small Animal Clinic to diagnose the severity of his heart condition and make sure he was healthy enough to undergo such radical surgery. The medical costs were mounting, and I wondered how much money was too much to spend on a cat.

I took Kenobi in for the heart procedure. Feeling like a mother hen, I waited in the lobby. Afterward, the vet gave me the rundown.

"He has hypertrophic cardiomyopathy," she said. In layman's language, Kenobi had heart disease. The vet took me over to a whiteboard and drew a diagram, explaining what was happening with Kenobi's heart.

I learned more about heart disease that day than I wanted to know. I tried to be optimistic, knowing his future may not be what I'd hoped. I clung to the positive. The vet said, if you have to have heart disease, Kenobi's was the best kind to have. That was a tiny bit of consolation as my own heart died a little that day. She recommended medication to slow the progression.

The doctor also believed Kenobi could undergo the femoral head osteotomy. Until that moment, I'd never considered that his heart murmur could prevent him from having the surgery. That would have been a death sentence.

How quickly things can change. A week earlier, I thought I had a healthy pet. The reality that my cat had two broken hips and a heart condition seemed surreal. I had a hard time accepting it.

I packed Kenobi in the van and brought him home. How difficult would it be to give a cat a tiny pill twice a day? Perhaps giving him his medicine would help me to remember to take my blood pressure pill.

That night I went on the web and consulted Dr. Google about hypertrophic cardiomyopathy. I made a conscious choice not to believe the possible dire outcome. Five years was considered the maximum lifespan for a cat with his condition. He was two; that meant he only had three more years to live. That was too hard to swallow.

Besides, I was more concerned with his upcoming surgery and making sure he survived the next week. I found an excellent blog someone hosted concerning cats who had undergone a femoral head osteotomy. The blog host's cat had also broken both hips and experienced the same procedure. There were many uplifting comments written by people about their cats. Overall, most of the cats had good outcomes.

We scheduled Kenobi for his procedure, also known as FHO. The goal is to restore pain-free mobility to a damaged hip. The surgeon removes the head and neck of the femur. I couldn't imagine removing that much of the femur and still having normal leg motion. I would have been happy just to have Kenobi walk without pain. The vet said he would eventually jump, which seemed mind-boggling when I saw him in such pain. At this point, even walking was labor-intensive. The only time he moved was to use the litter box.

On Saturday his walking declined dramatically, and he was in as much pain as when we had first taken him to the vet. Since our vet was closed, I took him again to the Small Animal Clinic at The University of Florida. They sent me home with pain meds to make him comfortable until our vet performed the surgery on Tuesday.

I dropped Kenobi off at the vet three days later, informing the doctor of the recent change in his other hip. They took X-rays, and the doctor called me on the phone and said Kenobi needed surgery on both hips, not just one. He said he had consulted with another veterinarian who specialized in animal orthopedics. Because of Kenobi's heart murmur, the other doctor agreed with my vet that the FHO should be performed on both hips in one operation, but he couldn't do both hips that day.

Because of Kenobi's increasing pain, decreasing mobility, and heart murmur, my vet made arrangements to have the surgery done the next day by an orthopedic specialist. He also wanted an anesthesiologist to assist with the operation. The cost was steep, and the risks were high. Several well-meaning friends suggested I should put him down.

"Never," I told them. God would provide the money even if it meant working overtime to pay for it.

The next morning, I took Kenobi in for surgery. After dropping him off, I went to Perkins. I was too nervous to go back to sleep. I sat and drank coffee for a few hours and read an inspirational book. Finally, the vet called and told me Kenobi was out of surgery. He said he had significantly decreased Kenobi's heart rate, and he did well. I could tell he was relieved the procedure was over.

That night, I called the clinic and asked how Kenobi was doing.

"He's doing okay," the nurse said, "but he's not eating or urinating on his own."

"Can I come down and see him?"

She put me on hold for a minute before replying, "If you make it brief."

I drove to the clinic and arrived within minutes. Not many people were on the road in the wee hours of the morning. The nurse took me to Kenobi, where he was resting in a small crate. As soon as he saw me, his eyes lit up. The tech opened the cage, and I reached in and stroked him gently on his head. Sweet purrs filled my ears. I smiled. He just needed to know I hadn't forgotten about him.

The next day I took Kenobi home. The vet prescribed morphine, and he wore a small fentanyl patch on his back.

During this time, my back started bothering me. Kenobi's recovery from surgery meant spending six weeks in a crate, so I was on my hands and knees, giving him his pills, cleaning his litter, refilling his water bowl, and reassuring him with lots of head pats.

My back tightened up, and then the tightness traveled down my legs. I went to the doctor to get some muscle relaxants. For the next few weeks, I walked more than usual, enjoyed Epsom salt baths—a first for me—and took Tylenol. I knew Kenobi's pain was more significant than mine, but it reminded me that we feel others' suffering when we care for them. We hurt for them and with them.

I loved Kenobi and esteemed his value even if others thought I'd spent too much money on him. I remembered that God cares for even the sparrow that falls from a tree.

Eventually, his pain subsided, and he became his old self again. Soon he was playing with toys and walking at a brisk pace. I was thrilled when he progressed to using the cat stairs I bought to get up on the sofa. Before long, he was jumping on the couch, lying beside me while I captioned, and playing with Anakin.

We figured out how to give Kenobi his pill twice a day. Thank goodness somebody invented pill pockets. I wrapped up his medicine in a salmon pocket, his favorite flavor, and he didn't even know he was getting it. And, for the next few months, life was good.

40

BREAST CANCER

Kenobi had his surgery in July. During his recovery, I felt a lump on my left breast near scar tissue from previous benign surgery. I didn't remember feeling it before. When I went to the doctor to get muscle relaxants, I wasn't concerned enough to mention it. I figured I'd bring it up at my next blood pressure appointment. I'd just had my annual mammogram three months earlier, and I was so focused on Kenobi, I didn't want to think about it.

In November, I went in for my blood pressure bi-annual appointment, and I asked the doctor to check the spot. She ordered a mammogram and a sonogram.

That was scheduled, and after the procedure, the radiologist said the mammogram was unchanged from the previous April. The sonogram didn't show anything ominous either, but the doctor said she could do a biopsy or an MRI if I wanted.

I asked for an MRI. I don't know why—the radiologist didn't see the need. I opted to have it done the first week in January. I would put it toward my deductible for the next year since I hadn't met it in 2016.

I'd never had an MRI, but I knew where The University of Florida housed the loud, intimidating machine. My daughter had undergone an MRI at seven when they thought she had a brain tumor. She did not;

she had a parasitic infection. That's what happens when you live in a third-world country and don't have access to clean drinking water. The scientific name is neurocysticercosis.

However, my dad died of a brain tumor. On the fifth anniversary of his death, my daughter had a seizure, and we rushed her to the hospital. September 19 is a dark day on my calendar. I'm always happy when the day passes, and nothing happens.

My appointment was early in the morning. I was surprised I could remember with such clarity the room's layout. Another woman with a friend soon joined me. We made small talk. Most people who get an MRI have something serious, so the mood was somber.

At last, I was prepped for the procedure. The familiar dinging of the machine brought back painful memories. As I lay motionless inside the MRI, I recited the stanza from one of my favorite songs, "Jesus is coming back again."

As the minutes dragged on—I had to stay in a very uncomfortable position for a very long time—I shortened it to "Jesus is coming." By the end of the longest thirty-plus minutes of my life, all I could say was "Jesus."

A week passed following the procedure, and I didn't hear from my doctor. I assumed everything was okay. No news is good news, right?

Then I received a phone call from radiology. "We need to schedule your biopsy."

"What biopsy?" I asked. "I had an MRI done instead of a biopsy."

"You haven't spoken to your doctor?"

"I had the MRI done instead of a biopsy," I said again.

There was a pause. "Have you talked to your doctor since the MRI?"

"No."

"She hasn't called you?" she asked me a third time.

Now I was in panic mode. "No. Why? Is there something on the MRI?"

"You need to talk to your doctor," was all she would say.

I jumped in my car and drove to the doctor's office. When I got there, I rushed up to the receptionist and told her about the phone call I'd received from radiology. She didn't appreciate my urgency.

"I could have breast cancer," I said, trying to get across to her that I needed to speak to my doctor not in a week but right then.

"You'll need to make an appointment," she said.

"I want to see her today," I insisted. I wasn't going to leave until I had an appointment that day.

The receptionist complied. I hung out at Starbucks for a couple of hours across the street from the doctor's office.

Finally, the medical assistant escorted me into an examining room. A couple of minutes later, my doctor appeared with the MRI report in her hand.

"Do I have cancer?" I asked.

She sat down and confirmed my worst fears, reading sentences here and there from the findings, throwing in comments about what certain things meant. Some of the words were unfamiliar. I don't think I understood much of what she read. I only heard one thing—I had cancer. I asked for a copy of the report when the visit was over and returned to my car. I sat in my van and called my mother.

"I have breast cancer," I told her.

"Do you have the report?" she asked.

"Yes."

"Can you read it for me?"

Although my shock kept me from comprehending it, I read the report to her over the phone. I only knew one thing. I had breast cancer.

❄ 41 ❄
THE FLYING CAT

I underwent a double mastectomy a month later. Twelve rounds of chemotherapy followed that. After a two-week reprieve from chemo, I needed twenty-five rounds of proton therapy. Two months later, I underwent reconstruction.

One of my greatest satisfactions in life has been that all my cancer treatments took place in one year. Once I met the deductible, my insurance covered everything.

After checking in the morning of my double mastectomy and undergoing some pre-operative procedures, I put on a hospital gown, and the nurse hooked me up to an I.V. The orderly pushed me down the hallway on a gurney and parked me near a clock. It was 10:30 in the morning.

When I woke up from the surgery, the clock said 10:45. As groggy as I was, it didn't take me long to figure out I'd been out for twelve hours, three hours longer than they anticipated. That meant there must have been lymph node involvement.

I will never forget lying on the gurney, waiting to be taken to my room, pondering how far my cancer had spread and how long I had to live.

My mind was well rested—after all, I'd just slept half a day, probably the most sleep I'd had in years—so my thinking was akin to crazy dreams on steroids.

Maybe I was going to meet my Maker sooner than I expected. That meant I needed to get rid of my teenage diary. Sometimes I would pull it out from underneath my bed and read a couple of pages to remind myself I was young once upon a time. I needed to clean out all that junk. I remembered those straight "A" report cards from high school. I kept them to validate I wasn't stupid. That was before I found my value in Jesus Christ.

I wanted to donate my old clothes to the Salvation Army. My daughters had been telling me to do that for years. I'd save them the hassle. I thought about my dogs and cats and wondered if they would miss me.

As the reality sunk in of leaving this world behind—my daughters, family, friends, and pets—I felt depressed. Loneliness filled my heart as I lay on the gurney in that dark hallway staring up at the clock. When would somebody remember I was still alive and take me to my room?

I soon realized I couldn't solve a single issue hooked up to an I.V. wearing a hospital gown. I couldn't even move, so I might as well think about something positive. I thought about how blessed I was. My mom and her husband drove down from Atlanta. One of my daughters brought me to the hospital. My other daughter was taking care of our pets until I arrived home. I thought about how glad they would be to see me, and I couldn't wait to see their happy faces.

I was thankful I had prepared for my arrival home. Who cared about what was underneath my bed or in my closet anyway. I had bought new bedsheets and coverings, and I thought about how comfortable they would be once the hospital discharged me.

My daughters and I had discussed that we needed to keep the animals out of my room in the beginning. That would not be easy because they would run in there every time we opened the door, and the cats would jump up on my bed. My room needed to stay clean to prevent infection. At the very least, I didn't want them in there right away.

I'm thankful for the friends that dropped off food, sent me cards, encouraged me, called me, and prayed for me. Even Facebook posts inspired me. My awesome daughters and extended family did whatever was needed. Nothing was too much trouble.

I took three weeks off from captioning, which was hard. I couldn't wait to get back to work. I tried to do as many things as I could to maintain some semblance to the world that was familiar to me. Life goes on even if it's different. During the chemo treatments, I remember thinking, especially toward the end when my body was in rebellion, that I just wanted my old body back.

We all have those points of bisection, before and after some significant life event. Much of the stuff in between is pretty mundane, but it's the dramatic moments we remember, and sometimes the lighter ones bring us the most humor.

When my daughters brought me home after my surgery, one of them insisted that I always have someone with me. A couple of days later, a good friend from my prayer group came over to be with me for a few hours when my daughter went to work.

We had just returned from a lovely walk with Sirius, and we were sitting in the living room. Out of nowhere, a cat that shall remain nameless came flying across the sofa and landed right on top of my chest.

My friend, who was a nurse, covered her mouth and almost screamed. I could read her facial expression—my daughter had appointed her to protect me from attack, foreign and domestic, and her failure would cause me irreparable harm.

I smiled. "It's okay. I didn't even feel it."

As I petted my needy cat, I was glad I'd decided to keep Faye, Anakin, Kenobi, and Sirius out of my bedroom until I healed. They were too unpredictable.

Strangely, animals know when there is something amiss. They do things they wouldn't ordinarily do, perhaps to get your attention, or become incredibly needy, or have other very personal issues—as I would soon discover.

42
ANAKIN'S EMERGENCY

A couple of weeks later, my daughter and I returned for a follow-up appointment with my surgeon. The news from the pathology report was disappointing. Two different breast cancers were in eleven of the fifteen lymph nodes removed. My doctor altered my treatment protocol to include chemotherapy.

In a strange twist of fate, the spot I had been concerned about initially was not cancerous but scar tissue.

I opted for a double mastectomy. That was an easy decision on my part, but the chemotherapy was another story. I hated putting poison into my body, and that's what chemo is—poison.

I'd never smoked, never took drugs, and hadn't consumed alcohol in over thirty years. To have poison infused inside my body was an abomination to me. I wanted a second opinion, so we set up an appointment at the Moffitt Cancer Center in Tampa.

A couple of weeks later, my daughter and I drove to Tampa. After reading through my case and accompanying medical notes, the cancer specialist recommended I have a CT scan of my lungs for the pleural effusion that showed up on the PET scan. She had never seen a pleural effusion caused only by surgery. Her concern about the pleural effusion was worrisome. None of my doctors had mentioned getting a CT scan of my lungs.

Afterward, my daughter and I sat in a restaurant in Tampa, mulling over the unexpected, disappointing consult. I felt beat down and overwhelmed. Why did the Moffitt doctor have so much concern about my lungs?

I was able to set up a CT scan for the next day. That was a pleasant surprise. I thought I'd have to worry about it for a couple of weeks.

The next morning, as I was getting ready to leave the house to have the medical procedure, I noticed our orange cat, Anakin, had something wrong with him. In obvious distress, he was groaning as he paced around the house. Amid all the cancer upset, I had taken him to the vet the week before for urinary tract issues and possible obstruction. He didn't have a blockage then, but I was sure he had one now.

With male cats, it's an emergency. I was afraid Anakin would die without immediate care, but I needed to keep my CT scan appointment. Radiology squeezed me in because of the concern raised by the doctor at Moffitt. A small window of time following surgery is recommended for chemo to start, and I didn't want to miss that window.

I called my daughter. She left work and took Anakin to the vet. Otherwise, I would not have kept my appointment. I wasn't going to leave my cat in such pain.

I learned later if my daughter had not taken him to the vet, he would have died. The vet hospitalized him, but they couldn't capture any urine. The situation was urgent. We transported him to The University of Florida Small Animal Clinic, where, with great difficulty, they inserted a catheter. We came very close to losing Anakin.

Cats have a sixth sense. My orange tabby knew I was sick, and he was worried. I wouldn't let him in my room, and following my surgery, I kept my distance from all the animals while I healed. His concern translated into a urinary tract infection that ballooned into a blockage. We had to leave him at The University of Florida Small Animal Clinic for a few days until he started urinating independently.

Initially, we thought he might have to have surgery to alter his male anatomy. I didn't want my poor feline to have a sex change operation. That seemed like a horrible thing to do to a male cat. Fortunately, after a few days, his condition improved.

We had reached a new low. I was worried about Anakin, and my outpatient CT scan procedure was subpar—to the point that the hospital wrote a report for what went wrong.

The CT nurse didn't know how to access my chemo port correctly. When she stuck the needle into the port, I felt excruciating pain. Later, they determined the contrast didn't go into my vein but extravasated into the surrounding tissue.

I didn't know what had happened. All I could think about was if I couldn't handle this, how would I ever get through a dozen rounds of chemotherapy?

The infusion nurses told me never to let anyone access the port but them. The CT nurse could have damaged the infusion site, causing a possible blood clot, infection, more surgery, and skin grafting. The chemo nurse was also upset that the CT nurse had not flushed out the port.

Following this painful experience, another nurse escorted me back to the waiting area. I broke down crying—the first time I'd cried through my whole cancer ordeal. A patient sitting across the room from me asked if he could pray. I nodded. God had provided a stranger to lift me up in prayer.

The next day, following the CT scan and endoscopy procedure, I hadn't received the results, so I was anxious for my first infusion appointment. Just the thought of that needle going into the port terrified me.

When I was able to speak with the Physician's Assistant, she said the lungs showed no signs of cancer, and the endoscopy biopsies revealed a moderate hiatal hernia causing my persistent heartburn.

Relieved, I thanked God for the good news. Otherwise, I would have become a stage 4 metastatic breast cancer patient. I still find it hard to believe I was a stage 3C with a clear mammogram and sonogram. No spread to nodes was visible on MRI or exam.

Despite my reservations, I elected to go with the recommended chemotherapy; eight Taxol treatments and four Adriamycin treatments. I'm almost three years out, so until I'm told otherwise, if people ask how I'm doing, I tell them the doctors are pleased.

And so is Anakin. Following his urinary blockage, we switched him to Science Diet, and he hasn't had any more urinary tract infections.

After the initial chemo challenges, my treatment with chemotherapy went well. I worked a regular captioning schedule for the duration of the Taxol treatment. I also allowed the cats and Sirius back into my room.

Once I finished the Taxol, I knew the next couple of months would be the hardest. I would receive four Adriamycin treatments spaced two weeks apart. The nickname of Adriamycin is "Red Death."

I'd also be living alone for the first time since I adopted my daughters—probably not how anyone would want to experience the "empty nest syndrome." However, I had a good support network—a one-another group who prayed for me regularly, a church I could fall back on if I needed something, and seven cats and a dog who wanted to take care of me with lots of purrs and tail wags.

The walks that Sirius and I made together during my chemo treatment brought me great peace and joy. I'd forgotten how relaxing walking can be. Frequently I would listen to podcasts or YouTube videos on my iPhone. Other times I would just think; plotting on my *Seventh Dimension Series.*

Kenobi and Anakin were once again spending most of the day on my bed, and Faye enjoyed pouncing through the revolving front door. She could never decide if she wanted to be inside or outside. The other cats, Lily, James, Twila, and Boots, never wandered far.

One of my daughters accompanied me to almost all my chemo infusions. Even though I wouldn't want to relive that summer, God's blessings abounded. He made sure I was never alone, and I felt surrounded by an invisible bubble of love.

I remember the day I finished my last Adriamycin treatment. My daughter and I went to the radiation oncology department and rang the bell.

Now I was ready for part three of my cancer journey—proton therapy in Jacksonville, an hour and a half away.

43
PROTON THERAPY

Life sometimes takes us to places we never imagined we would go. I'd put my ex-husband through medical school, and we had gone to Gainesville, Florida, for his residency in radiation oncology. Thirty years later, I would be treated by the University where he did his specialty training, at the UF Proton Therapy Center.

The fourth Adriamycin treatment had been merciless on my body, so we postponed therapy for a week. After four months, my hair had fallen out, food tasted terrible, I'd fainted, my digestive system was unruly, and all I wanted to do was sleep.

Since the UF Health Proton Therapy Center was an hour and a half away, I had to rent an apartment and stay in Jacksonville while undergoing treatment. I needed another week following my chemotherapy before I could even think about packing up and driving there.

On a hot Sunday afternoon in August, I pulled out of the driveway, and a somber mood filled my heart. I was sad to leave my home, my daughters, my dog and cats, and friends. Even though I drove back to Gainesville on the weekends, I remained in Jacksonville during the week. I was thankful I could attend church, but I missed my Wednesday night prayer group.

After arriving, I unpacked my bags and got familiar with the general area, found the closest Starbucks, and joined the local YMCA for five weeks under a special arrangement with the Proton Therapy Center. I wanted to make sure I got in my six thousand steps each day.

My goal was to finish the first draft of *Seventh Dimension - The Prescience* before going to Jacksonville, so I met my self-imposed deadline. I would have five weeks to edit it during the week between treatments.

No one could have anticipated one of the strongest hurricanes ever recorded in the North Atlantic would pummel Jacksonville during my treatment. When those dreaded weather reports filled the radio, T.V., and internet, I debated, should I stay in Jacksonville?

It was Labor Day weekend, a more extended weekend than usual. Suppose I couldn't make it back to Jacksonville from Gainesville? The doctors were very adamant about keeping the treatments on a specific schedule.

Since the Proton Therapy Center was part of The University of Florida, and thus a teaching hospital, the protocol used would later be peer-reviewed in case studies to make statistical comparisons of best treatment modalities. There was little wiggle room for missed treatments.

I certainly didn't want my cancer treatment records thrown out of research protocol due to flooded-out roads. Or suppose my daughters needed me? What if something happened that required evacuating from Gainesville? We had seven cats and a Border Collie. They would need my help.

I thought I'd anticipated every possible contingency, but a devastating hurricane had not been on my to-do list for preparations. The passage from Proverbs 16:16 reminded me, "We can make our plans, but the final outcome is in God's hands" (TLB).

After much wavering back and forth, I felt I'd be safer away from the coast. Gainesville is in the middle of the state. And another factor —a big one—was my Jacksonville apartment was up a flight of stairs and surrounded by glass. I didn't think it would be safe only a mile from the Atlantic. I drove around Jacksonville, picking up supplies on my way back to Gainesville.

In hindsight, I made the right decision. I later learned, if I had stayed, I would've been sitting in darkness for three days as the area lost electricity, and the Proton Therapy Center shut down an extra day.

In Gainesville, we never lost power, and I worked solidly for three days providing weather-related captions for all the states impacted by the hurricane.

We were fortunate. Most of my friends lost power, and we ended up giving away our generator gas to a friend. The gas stations in Gainesville ran out of recreational fuel, and we never used ours and didn't need it. Mother always said God never gives us more than we can handle. God's grace covered us.

Sometimes, I feel like, while time marches on, some moments remain frozen in time. My five weeks in Jacksonville is one of those moments.

When I pulled out of the driveway and headed to Jacksonville for my first proton therapy treatment, my biggest fear was that I'd be around gloomy cancer patients who were on their last leg before stepping into the grave.

Up until I went to Jacksonville, I had insisted on a few things through my cancer fight. I avoided negative people like the plague. I wouldn't allow my daughters to criticize me—even if they had every reason to—and I would not read anything on the internet about cancer before going to bed.

One of the reasons I had chosen to stay where I stayed in Jacksonville instead of the preferred housing for many proton therapy patients was I didn't want to be stuck with depressing people. I'd rather be alone and content than be with unhappy families.

I couldn't have been more wrong. The Proton Therapy Center had a full-time coordinator who made sure patients were well maintained. We had a luncheon every Wednesday, and the UF Proton Therapy Center invited the patients and their families. After a specially catered meal and a short presentation about some aspect of proton therapy, patients were encouraged to share from their heart whatever they wanted.

I soon discovered patients were being treated from all over the world—as far away as India and England. There were also get-togethers throughout the week at various restaurants, and the friends I made blessed me in many ways.

To my surprise, almost everyone was thankful and upbeat to be receiving some of the best cancer treatment on the planet.

Of course, some moments brought me sadness, like all the children I saw who had cancer. They required sedation before receiving treatment, and I'd see the technician wheeling them down the hallway.

In the lobby, the families waited with their siblings. I related personally because of what I'd gone through with one of my daughters when she was seven. We had spent nine days in the hospital at one point, undergoing a barrage of tests to rule out a brain tumor.

But I never saw a tear at the Proton Therapy Center. The kids were well entertained—with puzzles to work, art creations to make, and musicians who came and played the piano or the guitar.

Every week people graduated from their proton therapy treatment, and we all celebrated with them as they would ring the magnificent bell that hung in the lobby. We clapped and cheered and shared their joy. They had completed their cancer journey, and deep inside, those like me who were patients longed for our day when we, too, would ring the bell.

When I was waiting for my treatment one day, I struck up a conversation with a lady sitting nearby who was also receiving proton therapy for breast cancer. She said to me, "I have a friend who went through breast cancer treatment. She told me when she finished her treatment, she was depressed."

Neither of us had reached that point, but she said, "If I'm depressed, I'll know I'm not the only one."

At the time, I didn't understand how anyone could be depressed after a year-long bout with cancer. I couldn't wait not to need more diagnostic tests, needle biopsies, disfigurement surgeries, poisonous chemo, proton radiation, living in another city, feeling like crap, or paying thousands of dollars for medical treatment to save my life.

I wanted to sit in my chair again and caption with my three cats—Faye, Anakin, Kenobi—lying on my bed behind me and my border collie, Sirius, lying on the floor beside me. How could anyone be depressed once they'd finished?

44

LIFE AFTER CANCER

At last, my celebration day arrived. I'd had twenty-five proton therapy treatments, twelve chemotherapy infusions, a double mastectomy, and numerous procedures to set up treatment protocols after the diagnosis.

To celebrate ringing the bell, my mother and her husband came down from Atlanta, and my daughters drove over from Gainesville. My new friends I'd spent the last five weeks with, most of whom were prostate cancer patients, and their wives, joined me in the lobby for end-of-treatment photos. Even my doctor and nurse came out to meet my family.

Ringing the bell and listening to the chimes and everyone's applause filled me with overwhelming gratitude. I felt like I was the winning quarterback in a championship football game. I had endured and finished. In fact, I'd won. I could now join the millions who called themselves cancer survivors.

My mother brought me flowers, we hugged, and I cried. They had arrived earlier in the week, and I went to the beach to visit them for a couple of days. The weather had been disappointing then, but today, the sun shone brightly, the sky was blue, and despite my skin being a wee bit raw and peeling from the radiation, I was ecstatic to be finished.

Afterward, my mother and her husband drove back to Atlanta. My daughters and I ate a delicious lunch of coconut shrimp and rice at a local restaurant on the Intracoastal Waterway. Then we went back to my Jacksonville apartment one last time, packed up, and returned to Gainesville. A chapter of my life was over.

After my almost year-long bout with breast cancer, I had one question that lingered: "How do I live again?"

When I finished my treatments in October (I had reconstructive surgery in December), I shared my thoughts during a church Thanksgiving Eve service.

"When you go through cancer treatment, it's like you're in a safe cocoon. You are surrounded by helping hands—nurses, doctors, friends, and family. Everybody is there for you. And when you pray, you know that others are also praying with you. You feel secure in their love.

"Then, in a flash, when your treatment ends, your doctors and nurses are no longer there. You no longer hear their reassuring voices, see their friendly faces, or feel their healing touch. You are thankful to be done, and it's time to get on with living, but how do you do that? You aren't the same person anymore. The disease changes you.

"You're more aware of your mortality, you aren't sure what your limitations are, and you don't have your full strength back; yet, others expect you to return to your job and the life you had before. There is an unexpected vulnerability. You feel like if a big wind gushed up unexpectedly, it might blow you over."

My daughters were disappointed that I refused to cook my homemade vegetable soup for Christmas—a long-time family tradition. I just wasn't up to it.

I discovered that even though I wanted to get back to normal, I wasn't sure what normal was now. Could I overdo it? Would my disease come back if I did overdo it?

Cancer treatment takes a toll on your body, it takes a toll on your emotions, and it takes a toll on relationships. I didn't know what to expect. I wasn't sure how much stamina I had—to work, take trips, or even how much sleep I needed.

I remember doing my taxes the first time after my treatment. As usual, the software had far too many hiccups, and I sat and cried in front of my computer. I didn't have the stamina to get mad and keep on keeping on until I finished them. I wanted to quit.

Little by little, I did reclaim everything, like cleaning the pool and walking Sirius—something that became far more meaningful to me after my treatment—and I even decluttered the garage and sorted through clothes and other things I was never going to wear or use and donated them to the Salvation Army.

I knew I needed to work on my yard. The hurricane had torn down many tree limbs and branches. Despite picking those up during one of my trips back to Gainesville, much more needed to be done.

When I removed the cover of the pool where hurricane water had collected, I discovered a black racer had made his home there. We had a friendly encounter as I spent over an hour helping him to get out.

I'd work at it for a while, rest, and go back and try again. I think he eventually realized I wasn't going to kill him, and he needed help. Now we were working with each other instead of against each other. After a few more tries, he slithered up to the top and made his dramatic exit.

I was most thankful that during my cancer treatment, none of our pets died. My daughters did an excellent job of taking care of our seven cats and dog while I was out of town.

Kenobi had fully recovered from his surgery, and Anakin and Kenobi were buddies once again as they had always been. Kenobi's fur had grown back—he spent a couple of months half-naked where they shaved him—and we were able to manage his two quarter pills a day for his heart reasonably well. He looked and acted like a healthy cat again.

When we go through a life-threatening experience, one positive thing we can do is re-evaluate our lives—the good, the bad, and the ugly. I felt convicted that I was violating one of the Ten Commandments.

God intended for us to have one day of rest each week. Perhaps if I had gotten more sleep, ate better, and worked less, my body would have been better able to fight off those proliferating cancer cells.

I felt blessed I had not suffered from lymphedema or peripheral neuropathy. That would have ended my captioning career. In addition to no longer captioning seven days a week, I no longer captioned late night and early morning shows. That meant I had one day of Sabbath rest every seven days and a healthier sleeping pattern. I'd forgotten how nice it was to live like other people.

A few months following my treatment, we lost Lily, my daughter's cat, to a Pit Bull that roamed the neighborhood. My good cat neighbors buried Lily for me. I went over there looking for her, and they told me the sad news. They lost one of their cats also.

Until then, I'd not been happy with that dog whose owners lived two houses from me, but what could I do? Their Pit Bull would come over and eat the cats' food inside our garage.

One day I went to the Pit Bull house and asked the renters to please put their dog in the backyard. I was walking Sirius, and I felt uncomfortable that their dog was trailing us down the street. They weren't very responsive to my concerns, only answering the door after I knocked multiple times.

My good cat neighbors called the police after their Pit Bull killed Lily, and the cops dropped by and issued them a warning. That made a difference. I never saw their dog running loose in the neighborhood again, and they moved out shortly afterward. I could rest now knowing that our cats were safe.

45
ALASKA

My daughter returned to Alaska to work at the Echo Bible Camp in Juneau the summer after my cancer treatment, and I flew up to help out in the kitchen for a week. I felt blessed to be alive, and I wanted to give back. I took my computer with me, and during my downtime, I worked on the last book in the *Seventh Dimension Series – The Howling*.

When I first arrived, my daughter and I spent a couple of nights with an author friend and her husband. We took the Mount Roberts Tramway to the top of the plateau overlooking Juneau, hiked some trails, and ate the best rockfish I'd ever eaten.

As we window shopped around Juneau, I tried to open a garbage can and couldn't. Feeling stupid, I stopped and watched someone else. They made it seem like magic. When I tried to do what they did, nothing happened. The garbage can remained sealed and shut.

I was too embarrassed to ask my daughter how to open the garbage can—both my daughters already teased me enough—so I asked a street person, "How do you open this thing?"

He laughed. "We have so many bears, if we didn't have locks on them they would come into town and gorge themselves. We want the bears to remain wild."

I was glad I didn't have to worry about bears in Gainesville. Alaska is a dreamer's paradise, but far too rugged to make it my permanent residence—and far too expensive.

I ordered a pizza from a pizzeria, and when they tried to charge me twenty dollars for a medium-size pizza, I canceled my order and went to the grocery store.

When the camp session ended, I spent a couple of days alone in Juneau before flying back to Gainesville. The staff no longer needed help in the kitchen, and the only people remaining at the camp were the counselors and staff.

A few of the volunteers had an opportunity to take an overnight ferry up the coastline to see the new campsite in Haines. My daughter went with her cohorts to assess it, and I hitched a ride back into town. Then I booked a hotel and rented a car.

The weather turned rainy, and I never enjoyed myself more—to be holed up working on my book without any interruption in wet weather thousands of miles from home, and in Alaska—I suppose only an author could feel that way.

Two days later, I picked up my daughter in town, and we reunited for the return flight to Florida. On the last day in Juneau, we visited some local shops, bought souvenirs, and hung out. She wanted to go to a consignment shop—not my idea of fun, but we did, and she picked up a name brand jacket at a fraction of the retail price. I was impressed.

While I didn't see any bears or whales—or the Northern Lights which I had hoped to see—God blessed me with magnificent Bald Eagles soaring across the sky, incredible scenic views of the coastline, and a spectacular trek to the Mendenhall Glacier.

On the way back, somewhere between Alaska and Florida at thirty thousand feet, I had an epiphany about a plotline that I'd been struggling with for over a year. Now I knew how to tie everything together. My great Alaskan adventure had ended on a high note.

After the long flight back, my other daughter picked us up in Orlando. We returned home, and I was greeted by several of my four-legged pets. I was glad to be back.

When I woke up from a short nap, my daughter gave me the bad news. "There is something I need to tell you that will upset you."

"What's that?" I asked, my exuberance from my trip falling away.

"Faye is missing."

"Faye?" I repeated, and I realized I hadn't seen her in my brief time back. Faye was the last cat we'd adopted four years earlier. She was incredibly sweet and thankful to have found a home, and I admittedly spoiled her with too many treats. She had known hunger living on the streets, so she had compensated by overeating.

She loved to climb up on my chair's armrest and sleep while I read on my Kindle. She wanted to be near me. I was her savior in her eyes, especially after she injured herself in the Humane Society accident.

I wasn't gone but two weeks, and I knew she wouldn't have left in that amount of time—despite being upset because my daughter trimmed her nails. I played the possibilities over and over in my head.

I called for her from the front yard and the backyard. My daughter told me she had been gone a week and had searched the subdivision many times. She had visited the pound, the Humane Society, and alerted the neighbors about our missing cat.

For hours, I scoured the neighborhood. As midnight approached, I continued looking. I decided to put up signs, so I ran back inside and found a jpeg of Faye on my computer. She was lounging on the armrest of my chair beside me. After printing out the photo, I showed it to my daughter.

She glanced at it and said, "People will think you are missing, not the cat."

I didn't think about that, but I didn't want to spend any more time looking for a photo of just her. So I posted the headline over the photo: "Missing Cat, Please Call If Found."

After I laminated several bulletins and walked outside, I inadvertently left the front door cracked. I was physically and emotionally exhausted, but I posted all the bulletins before heading back to the house.

Then I saw Sirius romping around in my neighbor's yard. He'd always come back, but I wasn't in the mood to chase him. I called him and did everything I could to coax him to me, but he wouldn't come.

I stomped home, complaining under my breath about him being a bad dog in one sentence and then in the next sentence trying to convince him to return. He just wagged his tail with his tongue hanging out the side of his happy mouth.

I went inside, shutting the door loudly, and as I stood in front of the living room window, I watched as he pawed the grass and waved his tail. "Catch me if you can…"

His playfulness was too much this time. I knew he missed me and only wanted my attention, but I was worried about Faye. Eventually, he returned to his senses and came inside. This time I didn't give him a treat. I scolded him. If only I had known what was to come.

Despite all the notices I posted on Twitter and Facebook, and signs I put up at the Humane Society, our vet's office, and several places in our neighborhood, we never saw Faye again.

I reminisced about how Faye loved going in and out of the house all day. If I opened the door and Faye was inside, she would run out. If Momma cat was outside and I opened the door, she would run inside. We could never have made her a happy indoor cat. Faye hated being constrained and wanted to be free.

She had been a feral cat, but she quickly adapted to domestication. She loved being loved and never would have left us voluntarily. Something took her from us, and because I didn't know what, I was anxious about our other outside cats.

I thought about the felines we had lost through the years. Maybe we shouldn't let them outside at all. Perhaps we should keep them inside. While we don't have bears where we live, we have foxes, coyotes, hawks, possums, raccoons, and armadillos.

I did an internet search to learn about feral cats. I discovered that the life expectancy of a wild cat is only three years. Domesticated indoor cats live on average fifteen years. I didn't know the difference in lifespan was so significant.

I thought cats in the wild did a pretty good job taking care of their needs. As long as they had their rabies, distemper, and parvo shots, received their heartworm medicine, and had their annual check-ups, I assumed they would live to a ripe old age.

Many of our cats had, but some hadn't. They had disappeared. Now that I knew about the dangers to cats from wildlife, I wanted to keep our outdoor cats in the garage at night and progress toward making them indoor cats.

We started with Boots, the oldest at fourteen. Gradually, he adjusted to being pampered inside, but it took time and patience.

As with all my other cats through the years, he loves sleeping on my bed. Every day is a gift for him, and his days, while numbered, are still good.

As I write this, his appetite is lacking, and today I bought him fresh cat food from the frig at Publix. He still purrs when petted and is content. I'm thankful we've been closer to him and spent more time with him in his old, old age.

While Boots took kindly to coming inside, our heart-compromised Kenobi didn't see it that way. Kenobi decided from day one he didn't like Boots. Anakin wasn't crazy about Boots, but he tolerated Boots as long as Boots stayed out of his way.

I'd hoped Kenobi would eventually accept him. I worried about his weakened heart. His negative preoccupation with Boots couldn't be healthy for him. Anger is never good, but try telling that to a cat.

46
SIRIUS

After church on a sunny day in August, I sat in Starbucks, sipping an extra-hot latte as I read a book, when my daughter texted me. "Sirius doesn't feel well. I gave him a treat, and he didn't eat it."

My daughter was remarkably perceptive when it came to the animals—she just picked up on things more than me. My focus was totally off the book now. I immediately left, and on the way home, I stopped at Publix to pick up some dog treats.

When I walked through the door, he didn't greet me, as was his custom. I went into the kitchen and put the delicacy in a doggy bowl— wet dog food— but he only ate part of it. I was concerned.

I went into my bedroom, which doubles as my office, to set up my computers for two hours of captioning, and I called Sirius into my bedroom. He came in, but not with his usual gusto. I told myself I'd take him for a walk as soon as I got off the air.

He stretched out beside me on his fluffy pillow throughout my show. When I finished, I grabbed his leash. When I called him, he came, although he hesitated. His eyes looked like they had mixed feelings. "I want to come, but I'm not sure."

He joined me with a little encouragement, and I took him for an extended walk up to the park. A long walk would cheer up any dog that was in the dumps. That's what I thought the problem was: just a wee bit of depression.

Our trip started the way it always did. He was exuberant, sniffing here and there, checking out mailboxes and bushes and weeds where other dogs had been. I didn't notice anything wrong until we neared the park, and then he started to lag. He would catch a smell and begin to investigate it, but then pass it up.

Then I noticed he was having trouble breathing. That's when I realized he was very ill. Now I was frightened. We were a long way from the house. I needed him to walk, but suppose he couldn't? My heart raced. Why had I taken him on such a long hike? I couldn't carry him. I didn't have a car.

With much coaxing, he made it back, collapsing as he entered the front door. He'd have done anything for me. I had an upcoming show, and I messaged scheduling that I needed off. I gave him a bowl of water, and then my daughter's boyfriend, who was at the house, picked Sirius up and carried him to the car.

The three of us sped to the emergency vet, and the technician rushed him into the back. I sat in the lobby, reeling from shock, trying to comprehend what had just happened.

Besides pesky skin issues and dry eyes, Sirius had never been sick. How could my Border Collie suddenly not even be able to breathe? I hadn't noticed anything was wrong.

A few minutes later, the assistant escorted us into an exam room, and the vet joined us and delivered the bad news. There was excess fluid in his lungs and body cavity. That's why he couldn't breathe. They could make him more comfortable, but they couldn't save him.

I spent several hundred dollars on diagnostic X-rays to make sure. The vet said I could spend more money doing more diagnostic tests, like bloodwork, to determine the cause, but it wouldn't make a difference. All they could do was make him comfortable. Did I want to put a twelve and a half-year-old dog through medical procedures that were only diagnostic and not therapeutic?

I left the room, stumbled down the hallway, and leaned my forehead against the cold wall. "No, God. No." I'd just lost Faye ten days earlier.

I remembered how Sirius had pranced around in front of the house, egging me on to chase him. I'd just returned from Alaska, and he only wanted my attention. I told Sirius he was a bad dog. I had no idea my Border Collie would suffer a medical emergency so soon after losing Faye.

How could I tell the vet to "murder" Sirius, who had been completely healthy as far as I knew that morning? What if I'd not taken him on that long walk? What if I'd taken him to the vet instead? What if's will send us to the insane asylum.

I returned to the examining room and repeatedly asked the vet, "Is there anything we can do to help him?"

She reiterated her initial diagnosis. I could extend my dog's life for a few days, but he'd be suffering, unable to breathe, hooked up to an I.V. in a crate in the back. His quality of life would be horrible.

Reluctantly, I signed the papers, and they escorted us into a bereavement room. My daughter, her boyfriend, and I waited. I cried. Several minutes later, they rolled him in on a gurney with an intravenous catheter inserted in his leg. He was receiving oxygen through a face mask.

I'll never forget his sad eyes. He knew he was dying. Every cell in my heart cried. I'd given anything to see him romp across the neighborhood one last time. His mischievous proclivity was only a game. He loved me as much as any dog could love anyone. That was just his unorthodox way of getting my attention.

Poignant memories flooded my heart. We knew we wouldn't get another dog when Molly died, so we made Sirius an inside-dog. He'd lay beside me on his luxury bed as I captioned. Sometimes I would read him the first drafts of whatever book I was writing. He always approved.

He discovered a special love in his golden years for one cat in particular—Kenobi. They were both black and white, and his herding instinct kicked into full gear to protect our beloved cat who was slowly succumbing to heart disease. I think he knew Kenobi was sick. Even though he loved all the cats, Kenobi was his favorite.

I couldn't stop the tears as I kissed him. I told him how much I loved him—for the last time. When I could no longer bear to see his sad face through the oxygen mask, the tech administered the medicine. His life left him, and my bull-headed, fun-loving Sirius was gone.

47
HARD TIMES

One of the risks of flying after a mastectomy and lymph node removal is lymphedema. When I went to Juneau to volunteer at the camp, I wore my prescription sleeve in hopes that would prevent it, so I was shocked when I saw my swollen, distended fingers after I arrived. How could that be when I'd done everything the doctors told me to do to prevent it?

I was going to be in a remote part of Alaska, so there was nothing I could do but pray and perform manual lymphedema massages. When I showed one of the camp missionaries my swollen fingers, she gave me some lavender essential oil to see if that might help.

I'd never used essential oils before, but it smelled good. Psychologically, I felt like I was doing something positive. Over the next several days, I noticed an improvement.

When the camp session ended, I returned to Juneau and found a pair of arthritic compression gloves at the pharmacy to wear on the airplane when I came back.

The swelling dissipated after I arrived home, but not entirely, not enough to please my doctor, so I did daily lymphedema exercises over the next several months. Lymphedema can be reversed if caught early enough. My biggest fear was not being able to caption.

After I returned, my first show was reminiscent of the first show I ever captioned—WWOR out of Secaucus, New Jersey. Those deaf folks saw some funny captions that night as my inexperienced captioning fingers tried to write something sensible.

Between lymphedema and losing Faye and Sirius within a couple of weeks after returning from Alaska, I was sad. I was working on the sixth and final book in the *Seventh Dimension Series – The Howling*, but I struggled to focus.

I lamented that I might never fly again. I'd always be at risk for infection and lymphedema in my left arm. I worried about losing the ability to do my job. I wanted my old life back before cancer—not just a little bit, but completely.

One day, shortly after Sirius's death, my daughter texted me on her phone that Kenobi's breathing seemed fast. He was back in her room on her bed. My heart skipped a beat. When I finished my show, she brought him to me. She was right.

I called the vet to make an appointment. My daughter took him to the vet —I was on the air—and I tried not to worry. She called me reassuringly. "Thank goodness we brought him in. He needs his medications increased."

All we could do was extend his life with diuretics and heart medicine. Our lives now revolved around making sure he received his pills four times a day.

I bought chicken pill pockets one day by mistake—although I didn't realize it—and I didn't understand why he wouldn't take his pills. I had that familiar feeling that I'd screwed up. I was notoriously unobservant and probably bought the wrong kind.

Sure enough, when I compared the empty pill pocket packaging in the garbage to the two new packages I'd just bought, I'd bought the wrong ones. What would I do with sixty pill pockets my cat wouldn't eat? And how would I get the pills down his throat now?

Because I didn't have lymph nodes under my left shoulder, I was reluctant to put my hands near the cats' mouths. My daughter came to the rescue.

Administering medications to a cat is not like giving medicines to a dog. Kenobi figured out ways to "beat the system." We'd come up with new ideas—new treats, new methods, new tricks.

Unexpectedly, Kenobi decided he didn't like the salmon pill pockets. Then we discovered it wasn't so much he didn't like the salmon pill pockets; he'd figured out how to eat the pill pockets and not the pill. What would we do now?

I continued writing *The Howling*, forcing myself to focus despite my growing concern over Kenobi. I had written *The Prescience* when I went through breast cancer treatment, and that was therapeutic. Writing *The Howling* was similar in many ways.

When *The Howling* was published, I took a break from writing and began to garden—something I'd done when my daughters were young, but I'd let the yard go. We had a company that mowed and edged the front, and the backyard was natural. Some might even call it a jungle.

Years ago, I'd planted Star Anise. Now the bushes towered over everything, including my house. Whoever thought they could reach twenty feet?

As I worked in the yard, cutting back prickly weeds, overgrown brush, and hauling almost thirty bags of leaves to the street, I was thankful that I had the energy to do the yard work. It wasn't so much I liked raking leaves; I was just grateful I could rake leaves.

I was determined to reclaim my old life back after cancer and not to let my sadness over losing my animals keep me from being productive. I was thankful we still had Kenobi.

The little bit I did was a pittance of what was needed. The yard was like a jungle on steroids. Then one night, after showering, I noticed itchy, red bumps covered my left arm. I remembered earlier scratching my arm when I was on the air.

I didn't want to go to the doctor's office. That would be like throwing a hundred bucks in the toilet. I'd refuse to scratch it, and then I stoically convinced myself it would go away.

However, in less than two days, the rash had spread up my arm to my shoulder, chest, and stomach.

No matter how hard I tried not to let my thoughts go to cancer, they found a way. Did I have a recurrence of cancer?

The truth is, all cancer survivors in the back of their minds know it can come back, but worry can steal your joy. I wanted to live life to the fullest. I made an appointment to have it checked.

48
PROVIDENCE

"Looks like poison ivy," the doctor said. "Have you been around any?"

"I've been pulling weeds," I told him. I blamed my yard woes on my yearlong bout with cancer. I guess the wicked poison ivy took advantage of my extended absence.

The positive side was that I'd been blessed with a good outcome and a second chance—even if it meant pulling weeds from now until eternity.

The reality was, I'd let the yard go for too long. I needed a professional to do the heavy stuff that I couldn't do, but I didn't know anyone who would do that kind of grunt work.

"Maybe you should hire someone to take care of your yard." The doctor gave me a prescription for the rash. Thankfully, the bumps slowly disappeared. I was relieved to know I didn't have a recurrence. Just poison ivy, but were my days of planting flowers and pulling weeds officially over?

The doctor's comments upset me more than I realized. Was I going to let cancer steal one more thing from me? I couldn't fly because of lymphedema, and my doctor had discouraged me from working in the garden. What else couldn't I do?

And then God showed me something. Perhaps I didn't want my old life back. What if I reassessed my priorities and made some positive changes?

I began taking a Sabbath day of rest. For far too long, I'd captioned seven days a week. As my Mom used to say, "All work and no play make Jack a dull boy."

THE GARDEN

The next day, as I was driving on I-75, my daughter called me. "A guy is here to take care of the yard."

I hadn't called anyone about doing yard work. I mumbled something to that effect, and she said she would get his business card.

Later, when I came home, I found the card on the dining room table. I read the name—Heaven's Tree Service. God must have sent the arborist. After all, the doctor suggested I have someone else take care of my yard.

The next day I called, and the owner arrived with two ragtag men in tow to "clean up my jungle" as he called it in between quoting Scripture.

He used men from the homeless shelter as his employees. "I pay the men and teach them how to be arborists," he said, smiling. It sounded like a match made in heaven.

The men looked over my yard as I told them what I wanted, and I shared my bout with poison ivy. The owner pointed out several places where he said I had it, as well as poison oak. I took pictures with the camera on my phone and posted them on Facebook.

A few people posted comments, "That's not poison ivy or poison oak." By the end of the night, I had a whole collection of self-proclaimed experts who disagreed with my arborist. Surely my well-meaning Facebook friends must be wrong.

The real work began the following morning. I heard the visceral sound of the chain saw outside my bedroom window. Men's voices and footsteps filled my dreamy ears. I wasn't getting up at eight when I had stayed up into the wee hours of the morning captioning.

When I stepped outside a couple of hours later, horrifying shock filled my disbelieving eyes. Heaven's Tree Service didn't clean up my jungle. They raped my yard, power sawing the hand-planted bushes, not just the brush.

The owner came over to speak with me, wanting more money for various things not included in his original quote. Uncharacteristically, I gave him what he asked. I didn't want any more poison ivy.

Upset, I went back inside, telling myself everything would grow back. Why hadn't I gone out sooner and inspected the work before the arborist destroyed everything? I didn't go out again until they left.

At sunset, I noticed debris in my pool—collateral damage from the clearing they did. Darkness was approaching, and I needed to clean out the leaf collector.

Reluctantly, I squatted down to unscrew the top, and I pulled out all the leaves. As I tried to screw the cap back on, I felt a searing pain. I glanced down and saw fire ants attacking my ankles and feet.

I slapped at them, but that only made them more aggressive. The pain made it impossible to think. Why hadn't I noticed the ant mound before I stepped in it? I couldn't leave the top off the leaf catcher, and in the fading sunlight, I didn't have time to find shoes and socks. Besides that, I had an upcoming show.

I stood there, determined to screw on the top. When my feeble attempts failed, I cried out to God, "Please help me." Immediately, the lid sealed, and water filled the leaf catcher. The pump hummed in a regular rhythm as water flowed from the pump to the pool. Why hadn't I prayed sooner?

I jumped out of the fire ant mound, slapping at the hated insects. I grabbed the hose and washed the rest of them off. The pain was excruciating. Then I ran inside so I could do a better job. In the darkness, I couldn't see.

As I rushed into the bathroom, I slipped and fell. As I lay on the floor, I realized how fortunate I was not to have broken my arm or hit my head. I got up, turned on the cold water, and gingerly stepped into the bathtub to soak my feet. Twenty to thirty red welts were already appearing. I stood there as long as I could before my show.

The burning subsided, and I was able to caption without the throbbing pain. An obligatory commercial aired, giving me a break. Kenobi, my ailing black and white cat with a black circle on his right shoulder, lay beside me. He often took catnaps on my bed or sat near my feet while I worked. He'd get lots of head pats and love strokes when I wasn't writing, and he waited for those commercial breaks.

I reached over and stroked him, knowing someday I wouldn't be able to. That was always in the back of my mind, his genetic heart condition.

49
KENOBI

During a commercial break, Kenobi wanted to climb into my lap. As much as I wanted to hold him, I gently pushed him away. "No, Kenobi, not now." My live show was about to return, and I needed to position my fingers on the steno machine.

My captioning wrapped up shortly, and I went into the dining room to eat a steak dinner with my daughter. We didn't often eat together, and even rarer did we eat steak. Tonight was one of those occasional nights.

We were sharing a meal—nothing worth remembering. Suddenly I heard a squeal. I turned and saw Kenobi running toward us as we sat at the table, pulling his back legs limply behind him.

I jumped up from my chair and ran into my bedroom screaming. My daughter had no idea why I was hysterical. At first, she didn't see Kenobi. I was a poor example of heroism in a crisis. She was stronger than me.

"It's his heart," was all I could say. "It's his heart."

"I know it's his heart," she said.

But she didn't know that night we would have to put him down. She didn't know that he'd suffered a blood clot that caused paralysis—that there was no cure, no hope, and no way to save him.

For three years, we'd extended his life with heart medications. I clenched my eyes. To know something is going to happen does not prepare you for when it does. You are never ready for death—of your own or a loved one or a beloved pet. It's not normal. It's not the way God made things, and it hurts.

I remembered how he'd tried to cuddle in my lap one last time an hour earlier, and I had pushed him away. The world wouldn't have come to an end if I'd skipped writing a few captions.

"We need to take him to the emergency vet," I said. I ran into the laundry room and retrieved the cat carrier. My daughter put him in it maneuvering his limp legs underneath him.

We made the fifteen-minute trip to the emergency clinic in half the time as Kenobi whimpered. When we arrived, the tech immediately took him into the back. We waited in an examining room while they worked on him out of sight.

A few minutes later, the doctor confirmed my worst fears. "He's in a great deal of pain, and it will be expensive to treat him. In all my years of experience, I've never seen a cat fully recover. He'll always be paralyzed, and the chance of another blood clot is almost a hundred percent. What do you want to do?"

I cried as my daughter sat stoically beside me. She loved Kenobi as much as I did. We were different. I signed the paperwork to "murder" my beloved cat.

I pleaded with God, "Isn't there another way?" I remembered when he broke his hips three years earlier, and we discovered his heart murmur.

I sobbed. Seven years ago, I'd made my first visit here with Molly, our Jack Russell. Eight months earlier, we'd been here again to say goodbye to Sirius. Guilt plagued me for taking him on that final jaunt. Now I was back sitting on the same sofa in the same room.

I'd thanked God repeatedly for keeping Kenobi alive, especially following Faye's disappearance and our Border Collie's death. We knew Kenobi was living on borrowed time. Losing Sirius and Faye, Kenobi's sweet mother, a few months earlier devastated me. Never again would my beloved trio of pets lie beside me for hours on end while I wrote books and captioned. I thought about how lonely Anakin would be without his best friend.

I needed to quit crying so as not to alarm Kenobi. I was thankful I would get to hold him one last time. I consoled myself that Kenobi and Sirius would be reunited. Both had brought me comfort and companionship through cancer.

The technician brought Kenobi, wrapped in a blanket, to us. She placed him in my lap, and I held him fast. I talked to him as if he were a person. I told him how much I loved him and how sorry I was. I petted his little head as I always did and smothered him with kisses. I longed to hear him purr once more, but he didn't. He didn't have it in him.

When the time seemed right, we put him to sleep. He closed his eyes, and I felt his spirit leave—like a wisp of air, a breath, something I couldn't see, but something discernible, and then he was gone. His life flashed before me in that solemn moment.

I thanked God for the three years we'd had him following his double femoral neck osteotomy. He had done well, better than I anticipated. He had fully recovered, his soft thick fur growing back where the vet shaved him. I remembered how funny he looked, but he didn't care. Soon he was as mobile as any other cat, and his sweet personality returned once he'd healed—until tonight when his heart gave out.

50

A BROKEN HEART

"I want it all, and I want it now," the commercial echoed in my head. I sat back since my show was finished and focused on the wooden box that held Kenobi's ashes. I'd made my decision—I'd never love another animal again. My thoughts were interrupted when my daughter walked into my room and traced my eyes.

She pointed. "You're going to keep Kenobi's ashes there?"

I nodded.

"You've got ashes of dead pets all over this house. What are you going to do with them?"

I shrugged. I didn't want to have this conversation. "I might make a memorial garden."

She rolled her eyes. "That's creepy," she said, and she stormed out of the room. We were both grieving but in different ways.

Anakin, our orange-colored cat, had already inspected the wooden box. Did he know Kenobi, his best friend, was inside the container?

Was I creepy, keeping the ashes of all my pets? How many boxes did I have? What difference did it make to her or anyone? For once, I didn't care what my daughter thought, but I needed closure. Perhaps keeping ashes wasn't what I wanted to do. She could be right.

What if I made a memorial garden and buried the ashes? I could memorialize each one with a plaque. I'd promise years ago to Thomasina, when I found her lifeless body under the pool deck, that I'd make a garden where I buried her.

Until now, that side of the house had been a jungle. I wanted to keep my promise to her, but what about poison ivy? I was fortunate it didn't cause lymphedema.

I remembered when Rex and Shelley were my only babies. I'd made arrangements before they passed to have them buried in a unique animal cemetery where families buried their dogs and cats.

I had meticulously picked out their plots and had plaques made to mark their gravesites. The local newspaper came out when Rex died and featured him in a Sunday afternoon spread about the pet cemetery —with color photographs. My youngest daughter was little, barely four.

I didn't have the money to do that for my animals now, plus it took time and planning. If only I had been more organized. I regretted not taking the time through the years to do that.

I stared at Kenobi's box on my dresser. I did all I could for him, reflecting on the shortness and frailty of life. Someday the four cats I still had would be in a box. Our animals that we love and cherish just don't live as long as we do. One thing I knew—I didn't want to bury any more animals.

THE GOOD SAMARITAN

Kenobi died when Heaven's Tree Service was finishing up. I wasn't happy with what the arborist had done. I knew he had overcharged me, but he was convenient.

I showed the owner the side lot where I was thinking about putting a memorial garden. "How much would it cost to clean out this additional part?" It included the area where I had buried Thomasina years ago.

The arborist quoted me $400. I knew that was too much money for what I wanted, but I was grieving, and I feared poison ivy again. If I were to create a memorial garden for my pets, someone else needed to clear the weeds. I couldn't do it.

The next day the owner showed up with a new helper. The arborist introduced me to the guy and added, "He's trying to get a lawn business started, so he's tagging along to pick up some work."

I was cordial but made it clear I already had someone to mow the lawn, and I wasn't looking for anyone new. The men understood and began to clear the area—another humongous task—working late into the evening after the sun went down. I didn't know how they could see what they were doing. I was captioning and could hear them raking and carrying piles of debris outside my window. I told them I wanted to create a heart in a section of the area they had cleared. The head honcho asked for another $150.

"I need the money for the rocks and flowers," he said, "and you need to decide on what else you want."

Why was he rushing me? And did rocks and flowers cost that much? I gave him the money.

Later that evening, after they left, I walked outside and saw the containers of flowers. The heart shape came from a cheap piece of rubber that he had talked me into accepting. I didn't like the rocks either. They were rocks you'd see on the street. Nothing was enchanting about my memorial garden. Maybe when I planted the flowers, the garden would look better.

I went back inside and went to bed, mourning over Kenobi, the money I'd spent for what I didn't want, and feeling pressured to make decisions I wasn't ready to commit to. The arborist had sweet-talked me into paying too much on work below my expectations.

Besides that, I no longer liked him. I didn't like how he spoke to the homeless men. He didn't talk to them with kindness. He yelled at them, men down on their luck living in tents on the edge of society.

I initially thought the boss was helping them—giving them work and training to hone their skills and become more employable. He had told me he was a pastor, and he quoted Scripture better than I could. Had God sent him to help me? I was confused, depressed, and poorer.

But my poison ivy was gone, and my car that had died was running again. I had much for which to be thankful. Even in my grief, I could make a beautiful memorial garden, but what I saw in front of me was cheap and ugly.

The next morning I heard the doorbell ring. I went to the door, and standing in the doorway was the helper from yesterday. I started to tell him that I didn't need any more work done in my yard, that I could plant the flowers myself, and I already had someone to take care of the mowing, but he interrupted me.

He said, "I want to show you something."

I followed him outside, where they had been working the night before. The heart looked even uglier in the sunlight. Maybe the flowers would help. They had planted a few already. I didn't see them until just now, visible in the daylight.

"How much has this dude charged you for this work?" he asked.

I shook my head. "I don't know—too much. He kept asking me for more money."

He reached down and picked up an extra piece of the rubbery border. "He ripped this from his yard." Then he threw it on the ground.

"It isn't even new. Those rocks he bought cost maybe ten dollars, probably not even that much. He bought three bags."

He pulled out his phone. "I recorded him last night as we were finishing up. I want you to listen to what he said."

"Just fill it up with leaves," I heard the arborist say. "She won't know the difference."

"You want me to put these leaves back in the heart?" his helper asked.

"Yeah, it will make it look thicker, adding in the leaves. She's rich. We can fix it later."

The Good Samaritan waved his phone in front of me. "This dude is ripping you off. I want to know how much you've paid him. He's taking advantage of the workers he's using, paying them hardly anything, and then pocketing the rest. And besides that, he's not even doing the work. I did all the work yesterday. He didn't do doodly-squat."

He added, "I couldn't sleep last night, lying in bed thinking about the money you've paid him, knowing he's cheating you, filling up that heart with weeds to make it look like there were more rocks than there were..."

I don't remember what else he said. I went and got my checkbook to see how much I'd paid him. When I looked underneath the rocks, I saw that they didn't even put down a weed protector. They would just come back, including the prickly Smilax. I wasn't rich, and the owner's fake Christianity had fooled me. He was a wolf in sheep's clothing.

"I will remove all the rocks and put them on my porch," I said.

He pointed. "You're going to remove all those rocks? All of them?"

I nodded.

"I'll help you," he said.

"I can't pay you. I'll do it myself."

"You don't have to pay me, Ma'am. I want to do it. I want to make things right for you as much as I can. That guy ripped you off, and I want to do this."

We spent the next hour removing the rocks and putting them in a pile somewhere else until I had the time to place them on the porch. They would match the stones I'd bought for drainage.

Then we went to Home Depot. I purchased a ground cover, a garden border I liked, and Vincas. The homeless man contributed $50 out of his pocket.

We went back to my house, and he helped me to get started. We redid the border, planted the Vincas, put down the ground covering, and poured out several bags of creek rocks.

After a couple of hours, we finished. I was pleased with the beginnings of my long-anticipated memorial garden.

51

HEALING IN THE GARDEN

After Heaven's Tree Service left, I raked and bagged dozens of bags of brush—what they should have removed and didn't. I tried to get rid of the Smilax, a weed from hell, and pricked myself more than once. Anchored under the gardenia were dozens of Smilax greenbriers.

I purchased a new shovel and dug beneath the once beautiful plant to reach the weed's bulbs. I couldn't get all of the tendrils out, but I discarded many of them in the yard trash.

I mustered the courage, using gloves, to pull up the Virginia creeper that may have caused my itchy rash. Although the doctor said I had poison ivy, some people are allergic to that vine, too.

I wanted to drown my sorrow in something that required no brain power but lots of energy. As often happens, once you start working on a project, you soon realize it's bigger than you anticipated.

I went to the other side of my yard where Molly and Sirius used to romp. They had chucked up rocks in an area where I wanted to plant flowers. I began to dig up stones.

Then I noticed sprouting weeds where quaint walkways used to be. In the past, I'd spent a lot of money to spruce up the yard. Now I wanted to return it to its former beauty. I wanted familiarity —sameness.

I needed to dig up the rocks in the garden and relocate them to reinforce the rock walkways. I redid the area between the pavers by the back porch and next to the philodendrons.

Then I got brave. Suppose I leveled it out and moved the outdoor grill. I set to work, and things went well until the wheels snapped off. My daughter came to my rescue. None of it was easy, but I was determined.

I bought garden gloves to replace my holey ones and a few yard tools. I worked through the daily late afternoon rains. I dug up rocks mired in mud. The wheel on my wheelbarrow was flat. I borrowed my good cat neighbor's bike pump and filled it with air. Now I could use my wheelbarrow again.

The more I did, the more I realized I could do. I stood back and admired what I'd accomplished. I could do this. After cancer—yes, I'd let the yard go, but if I took proper precautions, I could work in my yard again and have a cherished memorial garden for my beloved pets.

As I removed more rocks, I discovered the most spectacular stones were the deepest. I filled up bucket after bucket and dumped the rocks in the wheelbarrow. After hosing off the dirt, I distributed them in the thin spots of the walkway. One day I dug up a soup bone, and then another one. These were the soup bones from my Christmas homemade vegetable soup. My dogs saved them, and the bones remained hidden—until now.

Some days the heat was so scorching I couldn't work for long without being drenched in sweat. When it became unbearable, I'd go for a swim. Other days, the rains came.

Several times I had to stop because of lightning. I never gave up, though, digging up rocks, laying down mulch, putting in borders, raking up leaves, picking up sticks, hauling dirt to fill in holes underneath the fence, planting flowers, pulling weeds, fertilizing, and trimming back over-exuberant flowers. Whatever needed improvement, I did it.

Soon I noticed something. I wasn't just removing rocks buried in the ground that I hoped to turn into a garden. I was removing rocks from my heart—big stones and small stones that had robbed me of joy.

Regrets and grief choked out God's love. My mistakes paralyzed me. I had failed all my animals in one way or another. Just as the Smilax vines had anchored themselves underneath my gardenia bush and were robbing it of nutrients to thrive, I needed to rid myself of negative thoughts.

I did that during my cancer treatment, but its progression is insidious. I reminded myself I always did the best I could with all my pets.

I found solace in the garden, in the dirt, in the rocks I dug up. The sounds of the birds and the swaying of the trees spoke to me. I thought about things that are hard to think about.

As I continued to dig up rocks, I found other things in the soil that didn't belong, like rusty nails from previous projects, perhaps the windows I had replaced a decade ago or the siding the past year.

I found worms and roaches and things that are common in a yard. Did I want them growing in my heart? I needed to let go and let God.

There was also the abandoned door a contractor from years ago had left behind. It lay on the ground—too heavy for me to discard.

I called the helper who had outed Heaven's Tree Service as phony Christians. Could he help me haul it to the dump?

I also had an old lawnmower rusting in the yard that hadn't been used in twenty years. Did he want it?

The lawnmower was beyond repair or practical usefulness. We took it to the dump. As we drove to Alachua to dispose of the household rubbish, the helper told me about his past. We had more in common than I realized. He was adopted like I was. And he had many stories to share—he was even interested in writing his own stories.

On the way back from the dump, my car overheated. We pulled off the side of the road into a fast food joint to let the radiator cool. We must have stopped five times on the way home, adding water every few minutes.

The next day I took my car to the mechanic. I had a cracked radiator, but the engine was okay. What would I have done had the homeless man not been with me?

One day as I was working, mosquitoes attacked me. That day I didn't get much accomplished. Some days I didn't have time to work in the yard. Little by little, however, I transformed my small plot of land. A garden emerged, and my heart healed.

I remembered the parable of the sower. As I dug up stones, I reminded myself that if I plant something here with all these rocks, the plants might multiply quickly, but eventually, they would wilt and die. I needed to remove as many stones as I could.

As I tilled the soil, I reflected on the last time I held Kenobi. I remembered how I felt his spirit departing. "Where did it go?" I asked.

"He returned to his Maker," the Holy Spirit whispered to me.

I remembered something I'd learned in college physics—matter can't be created or destroyed, only converted to a different form. I also remembered what the Apostle Paul wrote in Romans 8:19-21 (NIV).

> *For the creation waits in eager expectation for the children of God to be revealed. For the creation was subjected to frustration, not by its own choice, but by the will of the one who subjected it, in hope that the creation itself will be liberated from its bondage to decay and brought into the freedom and glory of the children of God.*

I examined the dirt and rocks around me. My hands no longer displayed the beauty of a fair maiden. Instead, they revealed hard labor, reminding me of Scarlett O'Hara in *Gone with the Wind* when she tried to woo Rhett Butler back after the Civil War. He grabbed her hands and held them up—her rough hands after working in the fields because all the slaves had left.

I was Scarlett O'Hara, and I was sweating like a smelly farm girl on a hot Florida day. I loved it. Could cancer hold me back? Never!

As I looked at the land God had given me, I saw beauty. Not the kind the world admires, but something different. Even rocks can be beautiful if we don't let them become stumbling blocks.

In Luke 19:40, when Jesus made his triumphal entry into Jerusalem on Palm Sunday, the Pharisees said to Jesus, "Rebuke your disciples."

Jesus replied, "I tell you, if they remain silent, the very stones will cry out."

I needed to prepare the soil—whether it was the garden in my yard or the soil in my heart. Digging up rocks, preparing the ground, and planting flowers brought me much joy. Did I believe that Kenobi and all of my animals were with their Maker? For the first time, after hearing God speak to me, I did.

Did it matter whether I kept my animals' ashes in the house or buried them in the garden—if they were with their Maker?

I'd loved many animals, but suppose another animal needed a home? Would I be willing?

❊ 52 ❊
JAMES PART 2

A few days later, I went to the store and bought a ceramic cat sculpture. I wanted to put a catnip plant inside the pot, but I couldn't find any. I purchased mums instead.

I placed the pottery where I buried Thomasina years ago. I promised her that night long ago that someday I'd turn that area into a garden. I found a photograph of her I could engrave on a memorial plaque. Eventually, I'd do the same for all my beloved pets—without feeling rushed.

The Florida summers can be wretchedly hot. With fall approaching, I looked forward to sitting on the garden bench reading on my Kindle. James loved to lie beside me, and he kept me company all summer as I dug up rocks and planted flowers and pulled weeds.

Occasionally, I'd reach over and scratch him behind his ear, and he'd thanked me with a delightful purr. Today, as I rested, I recalled a quirky event from a few nights earlier.

Ever since we lost Faye, I began putting Twila and James in the garage at night. I set wet cat food out to lure them in—although now they didn't need to be enticed. They usually would be waiting for me—but James hadn't come to me that night as usual.

When one of them didn't greet me, I'd start to worry. I called a few more times, and then I saw James, his all-black body barely visible in the darkness.

I picked him up in the street, lightly making a fuss that he hadn't come when I called. I flipped him over on his back, kissed him on the head, as I always did, and carried him inside the house.

"James, I think you're losing a little weight," I said. By now, he should be purring. Why was he so quiet tonight? I kissed him again, trying to initiate the expected response.

I didn't think much more about it but carried him into the garage through the house since I'd already shut the garage door. I set him down in front of his wet food and stepped back to watch him dig in. He had a voracious appetite, but he seemed hesitant to eat.

"What's wrong with you, James? You seem skittish tonight."

He looked up at me but didn't make any cat sounds. I went back inside but glanced through the door windowpane. Twila walked up to James, and James backed off. Was Twila hissing at him?

What was going on with my cats? I opened the door and examined James more carefully. Wait a minute. Was that James? If it wasn't James, who was it? Had I picked up a stray cat, hugged him, kissed him, and brought him inside my house?

The cat stared at me with confused, round brown eyes. James' eyes weren't that round. Boy, had I screwed up! I ran over and opened the garage side door and stood back.

The timid cat, appearing very unsure about what had just taken place, decided to do the smart thing. He strolled over to the door and walked out. I shut the door and looked at Twila. Her eyes bulged in disbelief that I'd brought a foreign feline into her domain.

I went outside again to search for my cat, and there he was—the real James. Relieved to have the right feline this time, I brought him into the garage.

The stray cat continued to hang around. When I saw my good cat neighbors a couple of days later, I asked them, "Is that your cat?"

They said, "No, he just showed up, and now he doesn't want to leave."

For the next two or three weeks, he hung around. When I'd call for James, the lookalike stayed on my cat neighbor's porch. He didn't seem eager to come back to our house.

My cat neighbors relented and adopted the homeless black cat. They fixed him, named him Peppi, and now he lives next door.

Cats choose where they want to live. They told me they'd confused James with their cat also. We talked about a distinguishing difference so that we wouldn't confuse our cats. James has a red speck in his eye, and Peppi doesn't. That's how we tell them apart. I was reassured to know I wasn't blind.

I couldn't wait for cooler days to arrive, and I always marked the official start of autumn by the arrival of the Sandhill cranes. They fly directly over my house on their annual trek to Paynes Prairie. As they gracefully soar in a V-formation, their guttural calls are unlike any other bird.

The first time I heard one was when I moved to Gainesville. The sound was so unique that I ran out into the street to see what kind of birds they were.

My long-time Floridian neighbors told me they were Sandhill cranes. If you ever hear them, you'll never forget their trademark call. Only a few birds have captured my audio imagination like the Sandhill crane.

I remember as a child hearing the Whip-poor-will in Atlanta. On and on, the nocturnal bird would sing, and the singsong melody of a mysterious bird I'd never seen enchanted me.

I haven't heard another Whip-poor-will in decades. Florida has the Chuck-will's-widow, which is similar in sound, but I haven't listened to that bird either in a long time. I imagine, like so many bird species, they are on the decline.

But for now, the Sandhill crane is not an endangered species, and they make their winter pilgrimage each year to Florida's wetlands. The following spring, they head back to the Northern Midwest, Canada, and Siberia.

I mark the official start of spring and fall by their arrival and departure. I find comfort in their cyclical migration, just like I know the sun will rise tomorrow, the day will pass, and the evening will come.

Life was less complicated with fewer animals, but I missed Faye, Sirius, and Kenobi. I missed giving Kenobi his pills and administering the eye droplets to Sirius.

Sirius also had skin issues that needed special attention in his senior years. We had gone through a myriad of failed interventions until we found a vet who came to my house and checked out the yard to discover the cause of his skin allergy.

With her help, we found an antibiotic that worked. I was thankful Sirius' scratching was ameliorated. I also no longer had to worry about all that dog hair—he shed so much hair I could have made it into a rug.

I didn't have to worry about hearing my dog bark at midnight when I was on the air. Strangely, I missed those interruptions.

Once I brought Sirius inside during a commercial break because he was attempting to imitate the owls. He probably would have herded them, too, if they hadn't been in the trees.

One time, in my early captioning days, I wrote a discrepancy report because Molly refused to come inside. She was like a fighter jet barking outside.

When I ran out to retrieve her, I spotted a snake toying with her as it danced in the starlight. How could I get rid of the snarly snake before it attacked my stupid Jack Russell—or me? I didn't think snakes even came out at night, but this one did.

My boss told me that was the most original discrepancy report she'd ever read. I should have known someday I'd be an author. The real untold story is what captioners do on commercial breaks. One time I killed a roach climbing up my stenograph machine. There is nothing more unsettling than knowing a roach is crawling toward your hands. What other stories I could tell....

53

HEALING OF THE HEART

At last, the Sandhill cranes arrived, and fall was officially here. Our church had started new Sunday school classes, and a friend called me one night after a particular class ended. She asked if I would use my captioning skills to transcribe her husband's course on the book of Job. I told her sure. I hadn't been to any of the sessions, but I was familiar with that Bible book.

Job was the first book I read from the Bible when I was twelve. My father had bought me a King James Bible. I remembered being elated that I could finally read some of that Old English. I didn't know there were easier translations or children's translations.

In my young mind, since the book of Job had only three letters, I thought it should be easy to read. I wanted to know what the Bible had to say about getting a job.

Of course, I've since read Job a few times and know it's not about working. Scholars say it's the oldest book in the Bible, and it's about a man who suffered immensely.

I didn't go to those Sunday school classes. I was still grieving from the loss of my animals and didn't want to be more depressed reading about poor Job, but God had other plans.

As I was captioning the first class from the audio recording on the church's website, the doctor shared a C. S. Lewis quote that transfixed me.

To love at all is to be vulnerable. Love anything, and your heart will be wrung and possibly broken. If you want to make sure of keeping it intact, you must give it to no one, **not even an animal**. Wrap it up carefully around your hobbies and little luxuries; avoid all entanglements. Lock it up safe in the casket or coffin of your selfishness. But in that casket, safe, dark, motionless airless, it will change. It will not be broken; it will become unbreakable, impenetrable, irredeemable. To love is to be vulnerable (Lewis, The Four Loves, 1960, emphasis mine).

Was that me? For the next several weeks, that quote lingered in my mind. Whether I was sleeping, driving, eating, or praying, God whispered those words to me. While captioning, I was most convicted. At the end of one of my late-night shows, I stood and walked over to the small wooden box on my dresser. I ran my hands along the engraved letters of Kenobi's name.

Was I refusing to love, refusing to risk loving again? Was I selfish? I'd vowed not to adopt any more animals—not because I didn't want them, but because I didn't want to be hurt again.

To love meant the possibility of being broken. The loss of Kenobi shredded my heart. The death of Lily, Faye, and Sirius over the previous year compounded the pain of losing Kenobi.

Christmas came. I made the homemade vegetable soup that I had refused to make the previous Christmas. I lamented that the last year Sirius was alive, he didn't get treated to his favorite thing in the world —beef soup bones.

I had no dog to give them to that Christmas, and I put them all in the garbage—and wept. The quote from C. S. Lewis had frozen me like I froze my beef bones to give to Sirius and my other dogs.

Spring arrived. I heard the drumbeats of a virus in China, and I saw videos on Youtube of people falling over in the streets. Could that happen here?

Soon the local and national news began to cover something referred to as the Coronavirus or Covid-19. I made a captioning brief so I didn't have to write it out a hundred times each day. I captioned Trump's big announcement to the nation addressing this new pandemic. The world changed overnight.

Until then, over half of my captioning was sports-related. March is a huge sports month. NBA and NHL are winding up their seasons with the playoffs on the horizon. March Madness is in full swing. Major League Baseball is gearing up with their grapefruit league and cactus league games. It's an exciting time if you're a sports fan.

Almost overnight, all professional and amateur sports shut down. I went from nonstop sports captioning to constant Covid-19 press conferences of mayors, governors, and the President.

Late one night, I came home from a memorial for a dear friend who had passed away, and the transmission blew out on my van. I suppose the one good thing about not having a van to drive during Covid-19 is I didn't have transportation to the store. My daughter used her car to run all the errands.

As I stayed home isolated, I watched people on the street walking their dogs. I had taken one walk since that last one when Sirius collapsed. I refused to walk again. But if I had a dog….

From time to time, my daughter had text messaged me photos of dogs at the Alachua County Humane Society waiting to be adopted.

"I don't want a dog," I told her. "No more dogs."

One night after I'd been in lockdown for a couple of months, the restaurants began doing takeout, and Bento's had their "buy one, get one free day." I drove up to Lake City to visit a friend with two mango Bobo teas. We hadn't seen each other in months. We threw social distancing out the window. I'm thankful God made us social creatures, not only with each other but with our pets, animals, birds—all creatures. Slowly, God was healing my broken heart.

I remembered the night I came home with dog food instead of cat food. We didn't have a dog. Why had I bought dog food? I took the dog food to the Humane Society, along with dog bedding and dog toys. On the way over, a homeless man with a dog was begging on the street corner.

Often I gave a few bucks to women I saw begging, but rarely did I give men anything. I handed him $10. "I'm giving this to you in the name of Jesus. Buy your dog some food."

As I pulled away, I looked at the seat beside me. I was taking all these doggie things to donate to the Humane Society. Why didn't I give them to the homeless man?

I ran my errand, but kept some toys back, hoping the man would still be there on my way home. He was, and I handed him two doggy squeakies.

I admit, I often find it easy to judge the beggars on the street, and I've seen videos and know some are not homeless. Perhaps I was influenced by a friend of mine in Australia who had recently lost his son to drugs. God, in this instance, gave me compassion for this man and his dog.

Whatever he did to put himself into that situation, be it drugs, hard luck, or poor choices, the man still had love in his heart for a dog; and for the first time, I longed for a dog like his.

54
ADOPTION

One day the homeless man who had worked for Heavenly Tree Service called me, needing a few bucks to purchase back his saw that he sold to pay a bill. I wanted more Smilex bulbs dug up in the back, and the amount I offered him was the exact amount he needed to get his saw.

When he arrived, he brought his dog with him. I was excited to have a dog in my backyard again. It had been almost a year since we lost Sirius.

I chuckled when I stepped in dog poop. The sixty-pound mix had a vast yard to romp in, and I stepped in "it." The familiar habit of finding the perfect stick in the backyard to scrape "it" off the bottom of my shoe and then hose it down was like an ole familiar pastime.

I missed not only having a dog, but I missed the doggie quirks that came with it. How could a homeless man's dog whose poop stuck to my shoe bottom stir within me a longing for another dog?

I remembered that trip through Bunnell many years ago when I experienced an overpowering longing. Could it be that God gives us animals this side of eternity to love while we wait for our future eternal home? In return, our furry friends reward us with a foretaste of God's unconditional love that we'll experience fully in heaven.

Every dog tugging at his owner on the street reminded me of Gypsy, Shelley, Molly, Rex, and Sirius. I couldn't walk past the dog food in the grocery store without seeing dogs' images on containers that reminded me of/looked like a dog I once had—a Shetland Sheepdog, a Jack Russell, a Border Collie, or a mutt.

Cat advertisements on T.V. pricked my heart. After being owned by several cats—we don't own them; they own us—I'd been cat smitten. We still had four cats, but I missed the ones we'd lost.

Each cat has a unique personality. Like people, they are quirky. One cat can't replace another. Our cats had entered our lives and left their mark, but I have to confess, Kenobi was special.

But what about getting a dog? The yard was empty—even of dog poop. I intentionally isolated my captioning chair from the rest of the house, but I never felt alone with Sirius and my cats beside me.

Late one night, I went to the Alachua County Humane Society's website. Maybe I did deserve a break today as that stupid commercial blared at me a year ago when I was captioning.

On the homepage, I saw the heading "Adoption." I clicked on it, and the subcategory "Dogs and Puppies" popped up. A hundred dogs of all shapes and sizes appeared. I scanned through the photos. I wasn't looking for any breed or mix.

I scrolled down the page and saw a photo of a dog the Humane Society named Peasy. I clicked on the picture of a Coonhound mix with long, draping ears and sad eyes. She was in foster care, and the information the family provided intrigued me.

The foster family said she was house-trained, got along well with cats, loved children, slept like a couch potato, and wasn't aggressive. I didn't want a puppy, and the Humane Society estimated her to be three.

I tried to set up an appointment to meet her, but a technical glitch on the website prevented me.

When I told my daughter I was interested in a dog on the local Humane Society's website, she contacted the family. Since she had fostered kittens, she could talk directly with the foster families.

We learned that this homeless dog was transferred to the Alachua County Humane Society from the Taylor County Humane Society in

January after being treated for heartworms in November. A family adopted her a month earlier but returned the Coonhound after two weeks, claiming a car rolled her. They said they chased her for seven miles and didn't want her anymore.

This traumatic history made me more eager to meet her. Older dogs are hard to place, especially after heartworms. That she survived being hit by a car with only minor injuries seemed supernatural.

With all the Covid-19 restrictions, it made setting up a meet-and-greet more challenging, but we set up an appointment for the following week. I learned as much as I could about Coonhound mixes. In the meantime, the foster family sent more photos. I couldn't wait to meet her.

55
GRACIE

Gracie

The day arrived. I hadn't left the house since the start of the Covid-19 lockdown, and because of the broken transmission in my van, we took my daughter's Corolla. Not having a van to transport my prospective new dog made me reconsider getting my van fixed. With 250,000 miles on my Sienna, I could have driven around the planet ten times.

It seemed wasteful to pour more money into such an old car with so many miles, but I loved my van. Sirius didn't get carsick in the very back. Hopefully, my new Coonhound wouldn't be prone to motion sickness.

Since we arrived early, I waited and watched as other families met their hopeful new dog. I'd never been to the facility when it was so quiet. Prospective adopters were the only outsiders allowed on the premises, and that was by appointment only. The onsite kennels were vacant. All the dogs were in foster homes—one unexpected blessing of Covid-19.

At last, Peasy arrived with her foster family. A young woman with a male companion helped the Coonhound out of the car. The minute I laid eyes on her, I knew she was mine. I saw a medium-large, short-haired dog that was unsure of what was happening and didn't want to be here.

I waved at the couple and strolled toward them as I eyed my hopeful new dog. She was even more beautiful than in the photos. After a few minutes, they let me pet her on the head. Those shy eyes and long, dangling ears stole my heart.

Uncertainty filled her hopeful face, and I reassured her that she need not worry. My daughter and I asked general questions, like what kind of dog food they were feeding her, and we inquired if there was anything else we needed to know.

After filling out the paperwork and paying the adoption fee, we headed home with our new Coonhound. I soon discovered poor Peasy didn't know her name. While I liked her name, I didn't feel like it fit her. I tried several variations, but none seemed quite right. I'd have to think about it.

When we arrived, I walked my new Coonhound around the house to the backyard. I was so excited I could hardly contain myself. Once the gate was secure, I removed her leash and set her free.

She immediately sniffed everything, checking out the fenced-in yard, all the nooks and crannies that needed investigation, and the jungle full of live oaks, water oaks, magnolias, and other native growth —including the unwanted thorny Smilax and Virginia creeper. She would help to control it as she romped around.

The Tarzan-like jungle had returned since Heaven's Tree Service had "raped" it the year before, but I had tamed the wildness and overgrowth into a quaint, secluded oasis. I imagined her thinking, "Is this my backyard?"

As if the realization sunk in that this was her new forever home, she took off in a wild sprint, running around the pool, chugging up rocks, long ears flapping, and romping on the stone pathway I'd created. I videotaped her joy on my phone and chuckled as a smile lit up her face, and her excited eyes sparkled in the sunlight.

After a while, I took her over to my small memorial garden. As I sat on the garden bench, she knocked over the small table beside it. She whimpered and tried to run off with her tail between her legs, terrified she had committed the unpardonable sin.

I soon learned she was terrified of everything—dog toys that squeaked, opening and closing doors—anything that startled her sent her into a submissive cowering bundle of fear with her tail between her legs.

After that unfortunate incident, I brought her inside. We put a doggy gate up to the sunroom to introduce her slowly to the cats.

Everything went better than I expected. Anakin, our orange cat, while a bit timid, soon was jumping over the gate so he could drink out of her water dish. Boots would take a little longer to adjust, but I knew with time, the chances were good he would.

Later that night, after I put my favorite new dog to bed, I went on the internet to look up Coonhounds. I concluded she was most likely a Treeing Walker Coonhound, hounds descended from English and American foxhounds. The American Kennel Club officially recognized the breed in 2012.

That was what she resembled with her mostly white coat interspersed with black speckles on her back and side. She had one sizeable brown spot near her tail. Her muzzle was primarily white, and brown fur surrounded her eyes and covered her ears. A few brown speckles dotted her head, and she also had brown specks on her legs.

During the following weeks and months, those sad eyes became rarer and rarer. I knew Gracie, as I named her after a few days, had a history of abuse, but for this Treeing Walker Coonhound, she had found a home where she would be loved and wanted. I quickly learned that Gracie would need time to become the happy dog I wanted her to be.

The first time I walked her started well—until she saw a car. She eventually grew accustomed to street traffic. She loved her walks too much to let cars take away her satisfaction of a long hike.

One day, we exited the sidewalk beside the road to go to the park, and a car approached, honking its horn. In one second, she reverted, probably experiencing a flashback to being struck. All the progress she had made was swept aside in one terrifying moment. I could hardly control her.

We hurried away from the road, and I embraced her in my arms. After a few minutes, she recovered to where she could walk normally on the leash.

One afternoon, my daughter invited a friend over, and I encouraged them to go out back and play ball with Gracie. I had bought a yellow tennis ball at the pet store. I'd tried several times to play with her, throwing the ball and urging her to fetch it, but she didn't know what to do.

Her lack of knowing how to play ball seemed out of character for a dog. Had she never had a puppy-hood? Perhaps my daughter and friend, being young, could entice her to lighten up and chase a ball.

Later I learned what happened. "Gracie wouldn't come to us at all. She was afraid of my friend," my daughter said.

I went outside and called my shy Coonhound. Gracie didn't appear, so I started looking for her. As I walked along the pathway between milkweed and shrimp plants, she appeared, moving in slow motion toward me. Her frightened eyes melted my heart. I'm convinced she thought my daughter's friend was going to take her away.

After a couple of minutes of hugs and kisses, she lightened up and ran around the yard. I threw the ball, but once again, I had to retrieve it. I'd have to keep working on teaching her to fetch a ball.

I was thankful that she could quickly become happy after being so fearful, and that gave me hope that someday, she'd forget all about her sad days of the past.

It didn't take me long to discover how much Gracie loved dog bones, although she didn't care much for the sweet potato bony treats I bought—what was I thinking when I got those?

She loved to take her chewy outside, lie in the grass, and eat it. Sometimes she would go up on the pool deck and lounge in the sun. I have a photo of her smiling with her eyes closed. Pure contentment covers her face.

One day I was working in the yard. I needed to use my hammer, but I couldn't find where I'd disposed of it. I chided myself for misplacing it. I was always losing things because I didn't put them back. As I was finishing up, I found Gracie chewing on the hammer.

I went over and retrieved it. Gracie knew she shouldn't have taken it, and a guilty, almost apologetic face reflected back. I reassured her I wasn't upset with her, but she'd done quite a number on the handle.

Sometimes I have to coax Gracie to come inside because she loves her big backyard. But it's nice to have her lie beside me when I'm captioning or writing, especially now that her eyes are bright and cheery. Once again, I have a dog and a cat keeping me company while I caption or write.

After I got the transmission fixed in my van, I took Gracie to the dog park. While she loved romping around with another dog, the other dog was a wee bit dominating. I realized as I observed her submissive behavior, she may not protect herself if an aggressive dog attacked her. I decided she could get all the exercise she needed in my yard. Besides, she had a hard time jumping into the van. I had to help her, and I'm a bit too old to be lifting a fifty-five-pound dog.

As the country struggles to come out of Covid-19, Gracie has been my doggie companion, and Anakin has become my face mask thief. I kept finding Gracie chewing on my face masks. How was she getting them?

A little detective work showed Anakin was the culprit. My orange tabby is probably the only creature in America that craves those things. I have to remember now to hide my mask in my purse. It brings back memories of my daughters when they were little, and I had to child-proof everything.

I sometimes wonder about Gracie's original family. Her reaction to hearing children's voices tells me she must have been around children, and I'm sure she had been around cats. She knows what a cat is.

When animal services picked her up, they also picked up a Coonhound with her that was probably her brother. The Humane Society said her brother was adopted at one of their weekend dog fairs right after receiving them and they were surprised that Gracie didn't get chosen. I told the volunteer God meant for Gracie to be my dog. He smiled as he handed me her adoption papers.

I've wondered if the Humane Society would release the name of the family who adopted her brother. Would Gracie remember her brother if she saw him again?

Whether that ever happens, she knows she's loved. It's amazing what a little love can do. If only the world could see the power of unconditional love. All we have to do is let the animals teach us.

56
ALL IN THE FAMILY

As I was nearing completion of this book, I spoke to my sister one night when she mentioned she would love to write Kitty's story. I encouraged her to do so and told her I would include it in my book if she did.

Here's my sister's story about her first cat—Kitty, a delightful interlude before the final chapter of *Tails and Purrs for the Heart and Soul*.

KITTY, MY SISTER'S CAT

When we lived in our small house in Marietta, my husband and I noticed this little black kitty playing in the tall grass of the power company's easement near our home. One day, I discovered the small black cat sitting on my front porch as I was leaving. I assumed it was hungry, and I gave it some leftover meatloaf and went on my way.

Imagine my surprise when I returned and found the same black kitty in my living room. My husband, with a sly grin on his face, and my cat killer Samoyed, Preacher, were intently staring at the furry little critter, separated by a baby gate in the kitchen. Before I could say anything, my husband said, "I saw a pack of dogs coming up the street, and I couldn't leave her out there."

Why would anyone want cats? I wasn't raised with them; we always had dogs, and I didn't want a cat. And I doubted that a pack of dogs was on the street, but I didn't have the heart to put her outside. That's how Kitty came to live with us.

Within a few days, I noticed Kitty was infested with fleas, ear mites, and worms. She also came into heat. All this reaffirmed why I didn't want a cat. Since my husband welcomed her, I made him take her to the vet to end all those awful maladies.

We still hadn't given her a formal name, but the vet needed a name to set up her chart. So, as are so many cats in the world, we named her Kitty.

Kitty came to live with us when I found out I was pregnant. Some minor pregnancy issues required me to rest at home for a few days. My husband had just picked Kitty up from her spay, so we had some quiet hours together.

During this time, Kitty claimed me as hers. Animals always know who they need to win over. That began over nineteen years of loyalty and affection that could rival any human and canine bond.

Throughout my pregnancy, Kitty would lie on the couch with me or sit on my shoulder. Eventually, she cuddled up beside me while sucking on a crochet blanket my coworker made for my new daughter. My husband used to tease me that she thought I was her mother.

As we were preparing for our daughter's arrival, Kitty took great pleasure in placing her stamp of approval on the various items we purchased. Shortly after we set up the bassinet, we discovered her using it. She was gracefully reclined, peeking back over her shoulder and peering over the basinet's rim. Her greenish-yellow eyes danced with her approval.

As with most cats, you always knew where you stood with Kitty. However, her excellent communication skills were not limited to tail slapping, low-pitched growls, or seething hisses. She'd reward men of great stature with a one-of-a-kind present.

She was capable of delivering superb kitty scratches with the pungent perfume of her anal sacs. No one ever said anything after receiving her fanciful gift. I often wondered if they knew the source of the smell. Kitty just wanted to let them know how much she enjoyed their affection.

When startled, Kitty could release those anal sacs with surprising force. One morning, Kitty came to visit us in bed. I don't remember what happened, but something startled her. She catapulted off the bed and expelled her acidic butt juice squarely into my husband's right eye!

In case you didn't know, the contents of a cat's anal sacs can turn an eye a shade of red you've never seen. I don't think Kitty ever gave it a cat wink that my husband was the main reason she could live over nineteen years—pampered and loved as most cats can only dream about.

My husband came in a distant second in Kitty's world of favorite people. Kitty made sure he toed the line, giving him positive and negative reinforcement until he was thoroughly schooled in "acceptable" behavior.

While I was pregnant, my husband's job was to scoop "Her Highness's" litter box. A neat, turd pile placed mindfully in the center of his bed pillow was all that was needed to convey that Kitty needed her litter scooped in a more timely fashion.

The birth of my daughter did not phase her adoration for me. She wasn't jealous in the least and was always very good with the baby.

As my daughter got older and became more mobile, Kitty took such obnoxious behaviors as tail pulling and full body baby crushing in stride. Only when she'd reached her fill would she give my daughter a much deserved, no claws out, pop on top of the head.

We moved into our current home when my daughter was quite young. A few years later, we installed on the front of the house French glass doors. There Kitty would spend the day sitting in my daughter's stuffed Winnie the Pooh chair chirping endearing little peeps at the birds.

That's where she always waited for me to come home from work.

I'd see her through the French doors, and as soon as she spotted my car pulling into the driveway, she'd run to greet me as I walked inside.

We had a little routine. I would scoop Kitty up in my arms, and she would flip over on her back. And then I'd carry her around like a baby, and she would wrap her paw around my arm. We did this every day until Kitty's last day with us.

The French doors also provided a peek into her reality—she was one territorial cat. Any time a neighboring cat walked by, Kitty would turn into a raging, maniacal beast. Spitting, hissing, and yowling, she'd slam her body against the glass doors, and the traumatized visitor would scurry away.

On another occasion, Kitty, who was not allowed outside, went to great lengths to squeeze through the front door. I didn't know what was going on until I saw a dog making a beeline out of the yard. My crazed black feline chased that poor dog into utter exhaustion. Mission accomplished, Kitty turned around and came back inside.

Most people don't consider cats to be brave creatures, but Kitty was quite courageous. I think she thought she was a black panther and not an eleven-pound cat.

Once a suspicious person was spotted in our neighborhood, and the neighbors called the police. When the intruder realized the police were onto him, he ran past our house into the woods. Our garage door was open, and the cops wanted to search our basement to ensure the vagabond was not hiding in there.

Hearing the commotion in the basement, Kitty charged down the stairs to check it out. My Collie, a gentle soul, preferred to remain at the top. She peered around the corner, waiting for the "all clear."

As Kitty got older, she began to have health problems, and she grew less tolerant of others. She idolized me, and if there was a god in her little cat world, I fit the bill. I could do anything to her—give her pills and clip her nails. Others—not so much.

On one occasion, my brother and his family were visiting, and Kitty was sitting on an open window ledge. My niece and nephew approached Kitty and pretty much pinned her in the window, leaving her no avenue for escape.

My nephew, standing in front of my niece and being the closest to Kitty, received the full impact of Kitty's wrath when my niece playfully planted her finger on Kitty's head.

I laughed when my sister-in-law blurted out, "That's why I don't like cats! They're so unpredictable. He wasn't doing anything to her."

I replied, "Her reaction was completely predictable. Her brother was the closest to her."

Kitty also dominated my poor Collie that we adopted from the shelter. When Masie arrived, Kitty chased her into the corner in a cloud of swinging legs, claws, and hissing yowls, much like scuffles portrayed in cartoons.

Kitty left poor Masie quivering in a huddled heap in the corner of the room. Two days passed before that sweet dog recovered from Kitty's introduction.

Kitty continued to assert her dominance, stalking Masie on occasion, surprising her around a corner, or, even worse, attacking her in a deep sleep.

On another occasion, I remember a phone call I received from my neighbor when we were on vacation. You know it's never a good sign when a conversation begins, "Hello, is Kitty up to date on her rabies shot?"

I came home to a blood trail that almost, but not quite, resembled a murder scene.

The hardest part of owning pets is that they don't live as long as we do. The same held for Kitty. When she was twelve, she had an extended stay at a vet specialist. Her diagnosis was Triaditis complicated with a calcified biliary tree. Her skin was yellow from elevated liver enzymes, but the vet thought they could save her.

A few days later, with Kitty on the road to recovery, we took her home as she sucked on her blanket in my lap. We were able to control her disease for the next seven years.

In her final year of life, she experienced a gradual decline. One day I noticed my very thin and frail Kitty seemed distended in her abdomen. I thought the worst, and an ultrasound confirmed my fears—

cancer in her digestive tract. The vet sent us home with meds to manage her palliatively and keep her comfortable.

After a week of coaxing her to eat and her abdomen becoming more distended, I decided I needed to do what was right. I made an appointment and took her in.

As we waited for the vet to evaluate her condition, Kitty did something she'd never done. She laid into me like there was no tomorrow. She tore me up!

After her outburst, the vet came in. Seeing the blood dripping from my hand and the scratches on my arm, she smiled and said, "I think she is trying to tell you that she's not ready to go. It's not her time yet."

Back home, we went. I nursed Kitty a few more days. Shortly after that, I noticed Kitty's condition was causing her pain. We could not let her go on. I asked the vet to come to the house, and I left work early to spend some quiet time with Kitty.

We had our traditional greeting, and she sat in the recliner by the French doors. While we waited for the vet, I held Kitty in my lap and listened as she chirped at the birds for what I knew would be the last time.

As I cradled my beloved, crazy cat in her favorite position, my husband let the vet into the house. In my arms and gazing into my eyes, Kitty made her way over the Rainbow Bridge to her forever home.

Thank you, Mom, and thank you, Paige, for sharing your tail and purr story from your heart and soul.

57
SWEET PEA

Sweet Pea

Years ago, I used to scuba dive. At no time did I ever feel God's presence more than in the depths of the sea. The sheer beauty in the world underneath the ocean convinced me that God was near.

I often wondered as I emerged from a glorious dive, why did God create such spellbinding beauty that few humans would ever experience? Unless a person dons a BC, regulator, and mask, the world beneath the ocean is a mystery. While a virtual reality gives a flavor of that watery world, the real experience is far superior.

When God created the animals, they had no fear of man. Many sea creatures have never seen a human; yet, the fish will scurry away when you approach.

Something happened after the original sin in the garden. Not only was the relationship between man and woman diminished with their Creator, but their affinity with the animals underwent a metamorphosis.

Occasionally when I caption news, I'll hear an unusual story about how animals that are enemies in the wild become friends. It's an anomaly; a peek into what once was and what's to come.

I'm thankful God gave us dogs, cats, horses, birds, and other species where fear has not hindered our friendship. I'm disturbed when people abuse animals, violate their trust, or disrespect the earth over which God has given us dominion.

Proverbs 12:10 states, "The godly care for their animals..." In the millennium, God begins the restoration. Our relationship with animals will be as it once was in the Garden of Eden.

The Bible says in Isaiah 11:6-9 (KJV):

> *"The wolf also shall dwell with the lamb,*
> *The leopard shall like down with the young goat,*
> *The calf and the young lion and the fatling together;*
> *And a little child shall lead them.*
> *The cow and the bear shall graze;*
> *Their young ones shall lie down together;*
> *And the lion shall eat straw like the ox.*
> *The nursing child shall play by the cobra's hole,*
> *And the weaned child shall put his hand in the viper's den.*
> *They shall not hurt nor destroy in all my holy mountain.*
> *For the earth shall be full of the knowledge of the Lord.*
> *As the waters cover the sea..."*

I find striking in this short passage that God speaks about a young child leading and playing with various animals—animals that are dangerous and untamed. Inferred is that the earth today is not full of the knowledge of the Lord.

How will knowledge of the Lord in the new heavens and the new earth bring peace and safety? How will that knowledge of the Lord be so universal that even children and animals will be protected by it?

When I was a child, God brought Gypsy to me. I promised her someday the world would know her story. It wasn't so much I wanted the world to know about my dog as I wanted the world to know about God's amazing miracle. God revealed His glory in our relationship.

Since then, for the last fifty-five years, God has brought many animals into my life, but Gypsy was the one that first showed me unconditional love.

Many years later, when the breath of life left Kenobi, my beloved cat, I felt his spirit departing, and overwhelming sadness filled my heart. I desperately wanted him back.

"Where did he go?" I asked God. A few weeks later, as I dug up rocks in my garden, still mourning his death, God answered me, "He returned to his Maker."

A body is like a slab of rock once the spirit leaves it. The corpse can't respond to stimuli. We can no longer communicate or love or have a relationship with a dead person or a dead animal.

The spirit is what gives life. There is nothing as final as a dead body and nothing so unnatural. God made us immortal, to live with Him forever.

When Adam and Eve disobeyed God, a pandemic erupted called sin. No vaccine can cure it. Despite all of our medicines and human accomplishments, we can't eliminate it.

We also cannot create life. We cannot give immortality to a life already created. Breathing life into an organism is the providence of God.

To think that a dead body will rise again requires a leap of faith. However, God gave us His Son, and after Jesus Christ died on the cross, He rose from the dead. Most people don't realize that over five hundred people witnessed Jesus in His resurrected body (I Cor 15:6).

God's Son is our example of a bodily resurrection and of life after death. The victory of resurrection is in Him alone. When Jesus died on the cross for our sins, He defeated death (Hosea 13:14).

Many years ago, when my father passed away in Atlanta, I was in Gainesville, Florida, cooking dinner, and my young, newly arrived three-year-old daughter from Nepal ran up to me with a photo of my father in her hand. She had picked it up off my dresser in my bedroom.

She barely knew him, having met him briefly twice. She removed the photo from the dresser, something she had never done, and handed it to me.

I thanked her and returned it to its special place. A few minutes later, I received a phone call from my brother.

"Dad is dead," he sobbed.

My father's death was not unexpected. We knew the brain tumor would take his life. I sat on the sofa, trying to absorb my brother's words.

I then understood why my daughter had brought my father's picture to me. On his way to heaven, Dad stopped here to say goodbye. God used my daughter to bring my father to remembrance. I later learned there was another part to this story of my dad's passing.

Long after I'd left home, my family continued to show dogs. Most had died over the decades, but Mom and Dad still had one dog left—Sweet Pea. I don't know where they came up with a name like that, but I guess she was as sweet as a pea.

Sweet Pea, my mom told me, loved to sit beside my dad on the couch. Dad was a couch potato as he got older, and the two of them kept each other company.

When Dad came down with cancer, Sweet Pea's faithfulness became even more pronounced. She hardly left his side, lying beside him on the sofa as he fought a valiant fight against his progressing disease. Over fifteen months, my dad went through surgery, radiation, and chemo, and Sweet Pea never left his side.

The brain tumor caused Dad to lose the ability to communicate. His words just got all mixed up, causing him great frustration and Mother even more so. Mom wanted to help him, but sometimes she didn't know how because he couldn't verbalize it.

The Bible says **before** God gave Eve to Adam as a helpmate, He brought to Adam all the animals (and even the birds) to name. Sweet Pea was Dad's canine companion. Sweet Pea's love for Dad didn't need verbalization.

While Dad struggled to communicate with us, Sweet Pea just loved him. Her compassion helped Dad more than we'll know because his disease didn't hamper their relationship. It just kept going, bringing Dad peace and comfort.

Sweet Pea always stayed in the living room, dining room, and kitchen. She had never ventured back into the bedroom. Dad passed away at the back of the house in the bedroom.

The ambulance transported Dad to the hospital following his death, and a few hours later, when Mom returned, she went to get Sweet Pea from her crate to put her outside.

Immediately Sweet Pea tore through the living room, down the long foyer, and back into their bedroom. She then stood on her hind legs and pumped her front legs to reach as high as she could to sniff the air above where Dad had collapsed.

Mom told me she knew Dad was above them, on his way to heaven. Dad had stopped by the house to say goodbye to his faithful wife of thirty-five years.

God allowed Sweet Pea a glimpse into the third heaven, a final farewell before an angelic messenger escorted Dad through heaven's gates.

For those who doubt my mom's conclusion of Sweet Pea's strange behavior, the Bible tells stories of animals seeing into the spiritual realm. In Numbers 22:20-33, Moses wrote about a donkey that saved his master's life.

Balaam, a man of God, was approached by messengers from Moab. The messengers wanted Balaam to go with them and curse the people of Egypt. The two groups sparred back and forth, discussing the situation. At last, the messengers persuaded Balaam to go, and he saddled his donkey and went with the Moabite men.

However, God's anger was aroused, and He sent an angel to block Balaam from continuing along the road. Balaam's donkey saw the angel with his sword drawn, swerved off the road, and headed into a nearby field. Balaam struck the donkey to get her to return to the way.

A second time, the angel stood in a narrow pathway next to a wall, and when the donkey saw the angelic being, she pushed herself against the wall and crushed Balaam's foot. Balaam struck the donkey again.

Then the angel went to a place where the donkey could not go around him, and when the donkey saw the angel, she lay down in the middle of the road. Balaam struck the donkey with his staff a third time.

Then God opened the donkey's mouth, and the donkey asked Balaam, "Why have you struck me these three times?"

Balaam replied, "Because you have abused me. I wish there were a sword in my hand, for now, I would kill you."

The donkey replied, "Am I not your donkey? Have I ever been disposed to do this to you?"

Balaam replied, "No."

At that moment, God opened Balaam's eyes, and Balaam saw the angel standing with his sword drawn straight ahead of them. Recognizing his shame, Balaam bowed his head and fell to his face.

In this Biblical story, God shows us that Balaam's donkey saw beyond the natural world into the supernatural and used the donkey to speak to Balaam.

What did Sweet Pea see? Did she smell the sweet aroma of heaven? Did she see the glory of the Risen King? Did she hear Dad's voice telling her to take care of Mother?

The Bible is full of stories—supernatural stories like this one revealing how God uses animals to protect us and help us. They are our companions and helpmates in times of need.

I expect God to restore all the animals He gave to Adam to name (many have become extinct). I imagine the new heavens and the new earth will have even more animals than in the beginning.

We already know heaven has creatures (animals) surrounding the throne worshipping our Lord that don't exist on earth. And because animals worship God, why wouldn't God resurrect all creatures?

I have a friend who loves cats, and she shared a dream with me that she had shortly after her second cat died. She told me she saw Jesus with a big smile on His face approaching her, and when He stepped aside, she saw her two beloved cats walking behind Him.

I've had many dreams about my childhood pet, Gypsy. She is pure white, and she's waiting for me behind a door.

God gives us longings that only He can fulfill. He blesses us with animals to love, and because our love is made complete in Him, our longings will be fulfilled in Him.

I believe someday we will not only be reunited with our pets, but we will even be able to speak to them. If Balaam's donkey can talk, God can make all animals speak.

Proverbs 13:19 (NIV) states, "A longing fulfilled is sweet to the soul."

Because God breathed life into animals and humans, that gives every living creature the ability to worship Him. In the new heavens and the new earth, our capacity to love will be as limitless as the stars.

God chose a magnificent animal, a lion, to reveal to us His glory and His strength. God referred to His Son as the Lion of the tribe of Judah.

When the Messiah returns, He will make all things new. He will make all things perfect. He will fulfill the longings of the righteous heart. He will restore the Garden of Eden. And I know—in fact, I am convinced—we will see our pets again, and I can't wait to hear the Lion roar.

EPILOGUE

Boots (on the back cover)

As I was finishing the edits of this book, Boots became ill, and I knew his days were numbered. For two weeks I hand-fed him, blessing him with an outpouring of my heart and reassuring him that I would be with him to the very end. The day came when he labored to breathe. I couldn't let him suffer. He was no longer purring, and I knew he was ready to cross the rainbow.

As with the others, my cat-loving daughter and I took him to the emergency vet, and Boots went to sleep in my arms. I felt God's reassuring love—"Boots is with Me now."

A couple of mornings later, as Anakin was lying on the bed with me, I saw a cat that looked like Boots in the dining room. The cat even had the purple collar around his neck that Boots wore. Confused, I tried to make sense of it. Perhaps it was James, and he had wandered into the house.

I rolled out of bed and walked into the dining room to check out the cat that looked like Boots but must be James. As I walked toward the door, the cat disappeared from the doorway and scooted underneath the dining room table. When I looked underneath the table , the cat was gone.

Perplexed, I asked God what He was telling me. I'm convinced God allowed Boots to appear momentarily in this dimension, again, validating that I would see all my animals in heaven. I hesitated to include the vision in the book. *People will think I'm hallucinating.*

A few weeks later, my cover designer sent me the back cover of *Tails and Purrs for the Heart and Soul*, and she had inserted the beautiful photo of Boots sitting among the flowers in the front yard. She selected that photograph over twenty plus animal photos she could have chosen.

I felt God urging me to include this final chapter of Boots' fourteen years as an epilogue. All of our beloved pets, including yours—are in the arms of our Lord and Savior until we meet again. I say, come quickly, Lord Jesus! Come quickly.

NOTES

8. TASHA

1. Online Etymology Dictionary. "Samoyed." https://www.etymonline.com/word/Samoyed
2. The Lutheran World Federation. "New Translation of the Bible in Northern Sami Language." 11-15-2018. https://www.lutheranworld.org/news/new-translation-bible-northern-sami-language.

ALSO BY LORILYN ROBERTS

STUCK AT HOME?

Children of Dreams

Children of Dreams as an Audiobook

The Donkey and the King

Food for Thought Cookbook

Am I Okay, God?
Am I Okay, God? as an Audiobook

The Door
The Door as an Audiobook

The King

The King as an Audiobook

The City

The City as an Audiobook

The Prescience

The Howling

The Castle

Tails and Purrs for the Heart and Soul

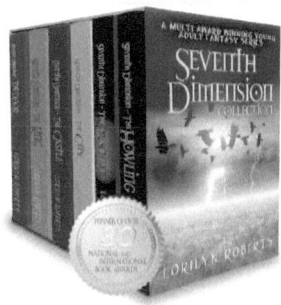

Complete Seventh Dimension Series Bundle

ABOUT THE AUTHOR

Lorilyn Roberts graduated Magna Cum Laude from the University of Alabama and received a Master's Degree in Creative Writing from Perelandra College. She has published twelve books for children, young adults, and adults that have won 36 national and international book awards. She has lived in Gainesville, Florida, for the last 35 years with many rescued animals. Lorilyn is a mother of two, a cancer survivor, and a passionate follower of Jesus Christ. You can visit her website at LorilynRoberts.com

www.ingramcontent.com/pod-product-compliance
Lightning Source LLC
Chambersburg PA
CBHW021054080526
44587CB00010B/247